Apprentices In Love

Apprentices In Love

MARK GIBBARD

MOREHOUSE-BARLOW CO.

New York

Published In England as
Dynamic of Love

Copyright © 1974 by Mark Gibbard
First published in America
by
Morehouse-Barlow Co.
14 East 41st Street
New York, New York 10017

SBN 0-8192-1166-4

Library of Congress Catalog Card Number: 73-89355

Printed in the United States of America

You learn to study by studying, to play the lute by playing, to dance by dancing, to swim by swimming; and just so you learn to love God and man by loving. All those who think to learn in any other way deceive themselves. If you want to love God, love him and go on loving him more and more; press forward continually, and never divert yourself by looking back. **Begin as a mere apprentice,** *and by dint of loving you will become a master in the art.*

St. Francis de Sales

I feel in my bones that I would like to write a letter. I don't usually write letters of 130 pages. My friends know that—they receive such scraps of letters.

Recently many people have talked to me about being human with their friends, their families, those they work with and meet, to say nothing of the dehumanizing pressures of our society, or of the growing populations thousands of miles away who do not have yet the bare necessities of human living.

This is not a book of answers. It is an invitation to explore.

Personally I doubt whether men and women are going to become completely human without some experience of the love of God. But this experience may come in strange and unexpected ways.

I have gradually come, and now I feel and trust I have finally come, to that conclusion. I have had my agnostic patches.

How many questions this raises! What reality does the word "God" stand for? What does Jesus Christ mean for us today? How necessary is the Church? What about life to come? What is the real value to us of prayer, contemplation and worship? We need to face these questions honestly. I am clear that it is an exploration by the

7

mind as well as by the heart. I write of things not so much experienced as glimpsed at and longed for.

How many friends, writers, and critics I have to thank! I hope that they will continue to goad and encourage me on this tough and fascinating journey.

MARK GIBBARD

Oxford 1973

CONTENTS

1 WHAT IT IS TO BE TRULY HUMAN

Most of us think we know what it is to be human. I thought I knew. My life was, and is, enjoyably full—studying, writing, traveling, speaking, meeting people. I had pretty good health too.

Then, a few years ago, my eyes were opened. Tired and with a slight cold, I went for a weekend to friends, a family in the country. The cold turned out to be pneumonia. My temperature jazzed about. I was a bad patient because I did not know "how to be ill." I was annoyed at missing work I should be doing. Gradually, thanks to patient nursing, I slowed down and something came through. I learned to take time at its own pace—and much more, as well.

As I left at the end of a couple of weeks, I shall never forget the members of the family waving goodbye, their parting smiles, smiles of accomplishment, of caring and of gratitude, as if they were even more grateful than I was. Sometimes a moment, a smile, discloses a dimension of being human which is skated over in our busy days.

So it was with one of the great men of our time, who was both a scientist of international repute and a priest—Teilhard de Chardin. A fellow scientist in China said:

Just to speak to him made you feel better; you knew that he was listening to you and that he understood you. His own faith was in the invincible power of love.

11

That quality was partly his temperament, but not entirely. It had not come easily to him. One of a large family, he had been brought up in the country, with a sheltered, perhaps too sheltered, youth. As a stretcher-bearer at the front, however, he experienced the nightmare of war. He knew questioning and doubt. Although he was unjustly treated by his Church and was forbidden to publish his writings, he was never embittered. His letters show how much his friends meant to him. He became a source of new hope and insight to thousands within and outside the Church. Through a wide range of experience he discovered what it meant to be truly human.

Obviously, we are not in his class. He is like an accomplished musician; we are nervous, fumbling beginners. We are mere apprentices in love, yet we share the same rich human nature with him. We too have something to give, undiscovered capacities. As someone has said, we are all "unexplored continents." This book is an invitation to a journey of discovery.

Our four needs

It is good to be living in an age which, probably more than any other, is the age of the ordinary man. Never have we had a better chance to get to know one another, to get to know how other people live, what they need, what we can do for them and what *they* can do for us. The jet and the television have made us next door neighbors. We are beginning to care more. As well as ourselves, we want others to develop their gifts and to become truly human. To do so, we must meet four needs.

First, clearly, there are material needs: enough to eat, a roof over our heads, good medical care. We still have a long way to go toward supplying most people in the world with even these basic material needs. Secondly, there is education—that kind of education which will unearth and develop our valuable capacities. And we must not forget that education is far from finished when school or university is over. By attraction or by repulsion our surroundings continually educate or miseducate us. Thirdly, there is the need for good human relationships. When we feel confident in people and they show confidence in us, when we give and receive friendship and love, something wakes up inside us, new capacities open up and blossom. We become more truly men and women. Almost everybody would agree that we have these three needs and that in this wide field all men of goodwill should discover how best they can work together.

Many people, however, would add that to become fully human we have a fourth need: *a real and personal relationship with God.* Let us always remember, however, that God is far more than a supplier of our needs. The fourth need is closely linked with the other three, particularly that of good human relationships. As you read on, you should often remind yourself of all four needs. It is about the last, however, that I shall write chiefly, because it is, perhaps, the particular contribution I can make toward helping men and women come to their full humanity.

The fourth need was well put by one of my favorite authors, Nicolas Berdyaev, when he wrote: *"Man without God is no longer man."* His words are all the more impressive because he was at one time an atheist—he knew all that could be said against God. Although born into an aristocratic Russian Orthodox family, he paid little attention to religion in his youth. All through his life he was active for social reform. While still a student at Kiev in Czarist days he was exiled for his Marxist activities. After his return he still moved in left wing and agnostic circles. Gradually, however, he was shifting his ground. "At a certain period of my life, which I cannot identify with any particular day, I recognized myself as a Christian and began to travel along the Christian road," he wrote. "In describing my religious evolution, I must insist that I came to religion retaining my freedom, and preserved it throughout my life as a Christian." He remained far enough to the left, however, to be given a chair of philosophy in Moscow for a short time after the revolution, yet he went on thinking. Because he refused to toe the party line, he was turned out of Russia. He lived next in Berlin and afterwards in Paris, where he taught at the Sorbonne. Out of long and varied experience, he could say, "Man without God is no longer man."

The test of experience

Are these words of Berdyaev borne out by experience?

Most of us can think of people, deeply and richly human, who, if asked, would say that this quality has come to them largely through communion with God in prayer. Many of them are men and women of acute, critical minds, not likely to be self-deluded. The philosopher, H. H. Price, in his Gifford lectures titled *Belief*, remarked that such people often seem to have "a certain serenity and inward peace, which others cannot help envying and even admiring." It looks as if there is something in it. In times of stress that peace often stands out more clearly than in normal times. The Jewish Austrian psychiatrist, Victor Frankl, in *Man's Search for Meaning*, the account of his experiences in concentration camps, describes how a genuine life of prayer enabled prisoners to overcome the terrible dehumanizing pressures of these camps.

On the other hand, Berdyaev's assertion would be challenged by many agnostics and atheists, and questioned, even, by some believers. Many, who apparently do not believe at all and who certainly do not pray in the usual sense of that word, are warmly human and live full, integrated lives, generous and self-oblivious in their service to others. However,—I can't help saying it—I think they are missing something.

I have now become convinced that almost all men and women have the potential capacity for a conscious, loving relationship with the reality of God. (What I mean by that I must leave until a little later on.) At least, it is certain that they have experiences very similar to a conscious relationship to God, experiences of being "taken out of themselves," of finding a new dimension in life through art or music or poetry, through friendship and love, through the magnificence and beauty of nature. For my part I find it difficult to draw a sharp line between some of those experiences and the realization of God's presence. What, for example, was Wordsworth writing about in his *Lines above Tintern Abbey*? Was it natural beauty or something more?

> And I have felt
> A presence that disturbs me with the joy
> Of elevated thoughts; a sense sublime
> Of something far more deeply interfused,
> Whose dwelling is the light of setting suns,
> And the round ocean, and the living air,
> And the blue sky, and in the mind of man:
> A motion and a spirit, that impels
> All thinking things, all objects of all thought,
> And rolls through all things.

Again and again I find myself wondering whether the capacity to respond to God may not often be a talent undiscovered and so unmissed in the great "unexplored continent" of oneself. That could easily happen, particularly to someone whose life is satisfying and reasonably successful.

Indubitably, other talents have been left undiscovered. That nearly happened to Kathleen Ferrier. She became eventually, as you may know, a wonderful singer. The daughter of a badly-paid village schoolmaster, she had to leave school at fourteen, had an unsuccessful marriage, and, since she had no children, an annulment. Although she was an able young pianist, her voice and gift for song went undiscovered until she was in her late twenties. If, a few years earlier, she had found deep happiness in home and children, she might have thought that she had everything she wanted, with no idea at all of her capacity for song and its development. What a loss it would have been for her and what a loss of joy for thousands of others. I think this is true of many who do not discover and develop their capacity for communion with

God. They not only lose something wonderful, but so do many others whose lives they touch.

The words of Berdyaev are also questioned by some believers, in two ways.

First, some say: "In theory I would agree that prayer should have this effect, it should make us more deeply human, but in practice I find it doesn't." What is the explanation? I am not quite sure. Perhaps it is that, even after years of praying, this capacity within us for a conscious relationship with God has not yet really awakened and emerged. Let us glance at another side of life. When we were children we knew in a way what friendship meant. We had our friends then, but now that we are adult, the same word "friendship" means something very different. It has depth, because something more has come to life within us. Often, the trouble with our praying is, I think, that it has not developed to a comparable depth. Somehow, our capacity for loving God has not matured. That doesn't surprise me, because many of us live in a rather materialistic kind of society which doesn't draw out this capacity. Also, perhaps we have never found anyone who has understood us, no one who has known how to help us. We've been like students without a tutor, like athletes without a coach.

Secondly, it is possible for those who have had deep communion with God to lose it. Sometimes their sense of God is gradually eroded or, even, suddenly shattered by, for example, a new, frightening aspect of the problem of evil. And sometimes, unhappily, "we can persuade ourselves that we are not hungry"—as it was put by that brilliant agnostic, Simone Weil, who came through so painfully to belief and prayer.

In contrast to all this, today, many are in fact searching to discover this capacity for communion with God. Often, they do not turn to the "official" churches, which seem to them spiritually dead. They look to new groups of Christians, who are certainly alive. Or they investigate eastern spirituality,

16

where they may learn ways of preparing themselves and opening themselves for prayer. Others experiment with a religious use of drugs. Some, like Nicolas Berdyaev, make their discoveries through reading and conversation and through their own explorations into meditation and prayer. All these things point to a hunger for God.

Through doubt to reality

The search for God is important and personal for me. Many people tell me they would like to pray but find it difficult to do so honestly. My own life, as I have said, has had its recurring patches of doubt. They have come again in recent years, but now they do not worry me too much. I have learned how to take them. Gradually through the years I have been led to the conviction—by faith or by insight, by experience or by intuition, whatever you may wish to call it—that even in the darkest days I am in contact with something or, rather, with Someone; and this Someone—I must give my reasons later on—is disclosed to me in Jesus Christ. He gives me strength and enough light, sometimes only just enough, to carry on from day to day.

To me, it is something like walking on the fells. If you love the mountains, you love them in all weathers, in sunshine, in a storm, and in cloud. Some days the clouds come down on to you on the fells. Then, you have to go carefully. You may have queer feelings, but you do not panic, as perhaps you did years ago when you first found yourself stranded in heavy cloud on unfamiliar mountains. In fact, nowadays you would not wish to have the mountains without clouds. Lovers of mountains do not always want sunny, cloudless skies. The great days on the mountains are those when your eyes rest on a patch of fresh green on a somber fellside picked out by a single ray of sunshine through the banks of cloud; or when clouds are caught in the winds and you see their shadows chasing one another over ridge after ridge; or again when the sun comes suddenly through the swirling, thinning clouds with an incandescent glow. So in our life of communion with God we cannot have the high moments without also the days of cloud, of doubt, of darkness. Some people may not run into these difficulties. But for many of us, our life of communion with God through prayer is, I think, aptly described in the words from the gospel "Lord, I believe, help thou my unbelief." Light and cloud, faith and doubt, coexist.

Our first times of doubt, however, are often not felt like that. They can be unnerving; I speak from experience. Perhaps that is why I always feel close to those who are having difficulties with faith and with prayer. It may help if I tell frankly how doubts first shook me, and have shaken me since. It is only gradually that I have come to see through experience what the darkness often really is:

> Is my gloom, after all,
> Shade of his hand?

I must go back to my first serious doubts. I started my academic studies with physics but changed over to theology to prepare for the priesthood. Then in a few months I lost all faith in God. That was serious and upsetting. Physics had always engrossed me, but I had given it up. Should I go back to natural science? The priesthood seemed impossible. I couldn't pray. A priest persuaded me, however, not to give up church altogether. As he said, it is hard to suppose that there is nothing at all behind mankind's experience of worship, even if the Church hasn't got it formulated very well. Many times over the years I've been grateful for his words.

It was not, as you might suppose, my critical biblical or theological studies which had brought on doubt. It was a misunderstanding of psychology. I had a passion for reading psychology. I read any book on psychology that I could lay hands on and find time to read. At that time it seemed to me that psychology had proved that there was no God, that the very idea of God was a delusion, a projection, a sort of idea which was somehow thrown up by my unconscious mind but

18

which corresponded to no reality. Like a mirage in the desert, it looked like refreshing water but it was nothing. "That then," I said to myself, "is the end of religion for me." But it was not. Gradually, I found my way. I saw that psychology can explain why most of us long for security and perhaps for that feeling of security which comes from believing in God. However, because psychology, like other sciences, delimits its area of study and confines itself to the field of the human personality, it cannot demonstrate whether God is real or not. It can only tell us what goes on inside ourselves.

Perhaps an illustration will make this clearer. A doctor could explain why we become ravenously hungry without food, but by his medical knowledge he could not tell us whether or not there was food in the kitchen to satisfy that hunger. He could tell us why we want food; he could not tell us whether there is food. Thus, the psychiatrist can tell us why we want this feeling of security which can come from belief in God, but psychology cannot tell us whether or not God is real. Dr. Stafford-Clarke, the distinguished psychologist, has written: "There is nothing in psychology which makes impossible belief in God." It took me rather a long time to reason my way through to that concept.

Faith gradually began to make a little more sense again. Then one day a fellow student said, "Look, we're going away for a holiday together in Cornwall. Why don't you come for a weekend retreat with me on the way?" It was not clear to me what a retreat was about, except that it was something to do with religion and with being quiet. I asked, "Are you so hard up for something to do?" I went, however, but in a skeptical mood.

The priest who led the retreat was an old man, who, even his best friends would say, was the most incoherent speaker in the world. I could not make out what he was talking about. What was worse, the retreat was in London near the Houses of Parliament and I heard Big Ben strike every quarter of an hour all through the night. The next morning, therefore, I wasn't in a very good mood and the old priest went muttering on. (Much later he became a very valued friend of mine.) I could not catch much more than a verse or two which he told us to read from the Bible. As it was all in silence, we could not discuss anything. At that time I was a great arguer—I would argue about religion from morning till night—but that was out. "Well," I said to myself, "I suppose I'd better read these verses." In one of them came the words, "Jesus had compassion."

At last I said to myself, "Well, at least this makes some sense. This is what the world needs. This is what men and women need—compassion, someone who will try to listen and to understand, to meet them where they are, to enter into their situation." Then I thought, "Whatever I do with my life, perhaps this is what matters most." I remembered also, with a certain amount of regret, that I had not been at all that kind of person. I felt compelled inwardly to write two or three letters of apology. Then I found myself far less tense about the God-question.

At the end of the retreat we went off. As we sat at the station waiting for the train, I said to my friend, "This hasn't been much of a success. I don't particularly want to see that place again," and then I added, "but perhaps something has happened to me." It had.

A journey of exploration

It was out of that retreat that my vocation—and incidentally my meeting other people in many countries in their perplexities—emerged, though it took a long time. I haven't always lived up to that invaluable glimmer of light given me that weekend. It has involved facing step by step, thinking about and coming to at least provisional decisions on many hard intellectual questions.

I would like you to explore in a deliberate and open-eyed way what praying, believing, and living can mean, as I began to do with a fresh impulse in that retreat. In our search we

20

shall encounter again and again Jesus Christ in the New Testament, in personal experience, and in the world of today. I have found how true are the words of the New Testament scholar, Rudolf Bultmann, "The decision of faith is never final, it needs constant renewal in every fresh situation."

2 PRAYING AND THE REALITY OF GOD

In the following exploration we might follow up on a clue from Erich Fromm, the psychoanalyst, who maintains that "the ultimate and real need in every human being" is love in its varied forms. The task, he says, is not only "falling in love," it is learning to love, building up love together. Loving, like other arts, involves some theoretical knowledge, much personal experience, and a deep, motivating concern.

The same is true of praying. I have become convinced of that. Praying also meets a human need. "Man without God is no longer man," as Berdyaev has said. Praying, like loving, requires some knowledge of theory, a good deal of personal practice, and a deep, motivating and persevering concern.

There is, however, a difference. In loving you can watch the other's face, you can feel whether there is giving and receiving, you can sense whether a real relationship is being built up. We cannot, however, see the God we pray to, we cannot watch the God we hope to love. Questions come to almost all of us: Is praying talking to ourselves? Is God a mirage in the desert? What reality, if any, is there corresponding to this word "God"? We can't speak about prayer helping us to become truly human unless we can say something reliable about what the reality is, lying behind this word "God." Those are difficult questions. We had better begin to face them at once.

The reality of God and the step of faith

When we talk now about God, we recognize that childhood ideas will no longer do. We do not mean some great being up in the sky or vaguely outside the universe. In the everyday sense God is quite beyond our "knowing." Strictly speaking, God is not a being, not a kind of third entity beside the universe and ourselves. We now speak of Him, rather, as Being, as One who penetrates dynamically all things, "in whom we live and move and have our being." He is in all things as well as Lord of all.

Perhaps some of those who say they cannot believe are rejecting not the true God, but an inadequate concept of him. As John Macquarrie tells us, "Criticisms of traditional theism are being met by the development of new forms of theism, and these in the long run will lead to a better and deeper understanding of Christian faith as a whole."

We cannot expect a massive demonstration of the reality of God. We cannot prove the reality of God in the sense that we can prove theorems in geometry. That our conviction about God often starts with probabilities, should not surprise or worry us. In many areas of life we have to act on probabilities.

Suppose you were in a firm considering opening stores in another part of the country, what would you do? You would send investigators to do some market research. They might come back and say, "There seems to be a seventy per cent probability that it will come off, or even an eighty per cent probability." They could never give you a hundred per cent certainty. If, however, you and your partners said, "We work only on proved certainties," then some more enterprising firm might go in instead of you and eventually drive you out of business. In friendship and love also we have to start with probabilities not certainties. Even natural scientists, who are thought to be hardheaded, also have to base their hypotheses on probabilities. They built their hypotheses on observations made in a necessarily limited range of space or time. They then assume, until evidence to the contrary turns up, that these hypotheses apply even in extremely remote spaces and in past and future time, they cannot investigate. Although the vast superstructure of scientific hypotheses rests on the assumption that "the whole of nature is in certain ways uniform," it is an assumption that can be no more than a high probability.

One of Christendom's great theologians, Joseph Butler, once wrote, "Probability is the very guide of life." There is nothing exceptional, therefore, in starting with probabilities, as we take first steps towards belief in God. What we begin to accept on probabilities may become, through growing experience, a deep conviction. The philosopher John Hick has said that for a man of prayer God is not "an inferred entity but an experienced personal presence." That does not mean that even for those who are only just starting out, there are *no* reasons for believing in God.

I would say that there are at least three pointers towards the reality of God: the observation of nature, the ethical character of man, and the fact of spiritual experience. Some people will find one, some another, more impressive.

First, *the observation of nature itself* is a pointer. When we look at nature, we detect certain sequences, regularities, and patterns. That, presumably, is what Bertrand Russell meant in his autobiography when he wrote that "number holds sway over flux." The stars, for instance, move in a regular way, so that we forecast accurately their future positions. Other examples may occur to us from the life cycle of living creatures. Or we may consider evolution, in some form, now more or less universally accepted. Although within the evolutionary process there are strange dead ends, clearly there is a general trend from inanimate nature through the vegetable kingdom, the amoeba, all the animal kingdom, up to man as we know him, to *homo sapiens*. We cannot see further. In each example, some rationality within us, something deep, asks the question insistently, "Why this orderliness? Why this particular development?" We can't rest, I think, with an evasive "Don't know; no reply." We find ourselves faced with a choice, although no one can give us an incontrovertible answer to it, either "It's a fluke; it has turned out this way by chance," or "There is some unknown factor, some purposefulness within the mystery, some kind of designing, behind what we observe." For me, the second answer seems much more likely: nature provides a pointer towards the reality of God.

The second indication, one which impressed the philosopher Immanuel Kant, comes from *our observation of the ethical character of man.* The majority of people seem at times to be conscious within themselves of a sense of right and wrong. By reason or by intuition, they are convinced that a certain action is right and ought to be done, even if it brings unpopularity and perhaps great hardship. They are equally convinced that another action is wrong and ought not to be done, even though it would never be found out. Their ideas of what actually is right and wrong differ widely. These ideas also change, and rightly change, with further knowledge and experience. Change, however, does not affect the main point, that there is in men and women a sense of right and wrong. For clarification, we might note that while people's tastes for particular foods differ and change with the passing years, the reality of their hunger and of the need to meet it does not alter.

The ethical sense, the sense of right and wrong, cannot be completely explained away by social conditioning, because men and women have often behaved contrary to the forces of social conditioning, because of their inward ethical sense. On the other hand, it cannot be completely accounted for by psychology. Psychology can show us something of the process by which these ethical convictions are built up, but psychology itself, because of the self-imposed limitations of its field of study, cannot judge the value of these convictions nor say what ultimate reality is behind them. Many careful observers of ethical behavior have thought and still think that there is an unknown factor, a supreme source of ethical insight and power within us, leading us on. I agree with them.

The third pointer is *spiritual experience*. Millions of people all over the world have claimed that through prayer they have encountered the reality of God. I do not refer to very exceptional experiences. I mean, rather, a sense of the presence of God, or a sense that God takes hold of some events in our lives and in his wisdom and love shapes and reshapes them. Such experiences are not uncommon. They are normally clearest among the great men and women of prayer: St. Francis of Assisi, St. Teresa of Avila, William Temple; but they also occur in the lives of many ordinary people. While we may learn more about that from those who have gone more profoundly into prayer, just as we may come to a deeper understanding of music through Bach, Beethoven, Elgar, and other great composers, we all can have a part in this way of exploring the divine reality and in sharing our insights with others.

Of course, some people may have been mistaken or deluded in prayer, just as others think they are in love, when they are not, but that does not mean that all love or most love is a delusion. Many men and women of prayer—St. Thomas Aquinas, Dietrich Bonhoeffer, Evelyn Underhill, John Baillie, to name a few—were not victims of delusion. They were people of balanced character and acute intellect.

Strange and fanatical acts have been committed, it is true, by men of prayer, as in the Spanish Inquisition and other religious persecutions. On balance, however, immensely good things have come through prayer. One example will suffice—and that from the Jewish faith. A thousand years or so before Christ, the Jewish people were, it seems, much like the Semitic tribes around them, primitive in their religious beliefs, and in their practice excessively concerned about details of worship and sacrifice, and far too little about social justice and integrity. The transformation of the Jewish people came

27

through a succession of remarkable men of prayer between about 750 and 550 B.C., whom we call "prophets." It was through their influence that the Hebrews accepted a monotheism of a kind unparalleled in the ancient world, trusting in and loyal to the One God who cared above all for honesty, love, and mercy. We can read at first hand the authentic words of these prophets.

One of the first of them was Amos, a farmer. In his prayer he received a strong impulse to go to the royal sanctuary. God, he there proclaimed, was not a national god of the Hebrews, but the Lord of the whole earth. Amos denounced the priests' preoccupation with the trifling details of the sanctuary worship. His voice rang out demanding social justice and love of brother men.

Such a message needed courage, because prophets like Amos were working against the entrenched opposition of state and "official" church. They had to have immense perseverance to carry through the necessary changes. They themselves were sure that courage and perseverance came to them through their contact with that reality we call God.

This is only one of many examples. The supreme example is, of course, the life and influence of Jesus, for, whatever we may accept or think about him, indisputably He himself was convinced that the inspiration and strength for all He did came ultimately from God. That and all the vast range of religious experience constitute the third pointer.

Those pointers are, however, only pointers. They will not compel anyone to believe. They will only indicate a direction to be explored. There are great difficulties in the way, such as the problem of evil, which we shall glance at in the next chapter. Those do not, in my opinion, inhibit exploration. It is up to each person to decide for himself whether to take a further step. That is not antirational. It goes in the direction of observation and reason. It is the step of inquiring faith. It seems to me that if we are never going to explore, never take a step beyond observation, never run a calculated risk, our lives are likely to be dull as well as impoverished.

The step of faith is not very different from the step of love. In both, it seems to me, we must keep our eyes wide open, we must reflect, we must weigh things and then have courage to go ahead. Erich Fromm has written: "To love means to commit oneself without guarantee, to give oneself completely in the hope that our love will produce love in the loved one. Love is an act of faith, and whatever is of little faith is also of little love."

What kind of God?

Before we go ahead with our exploration we had better look, although far too briefly, at two preliminary questions.

Is God "personal" or an impersonal force? Notice, by using the word "personal," I do not mean that He is a celestial emperor. I only mean that He can make personal relationships with us. Strictly speaking, personal language is used, only because it is the least inadequate language. What we are speaking about is beyond words. If we can make personal relationships with one another, surely He, the Source of our being, can do so. The source of water is always higher than the level of the water. The relationships He makes with us cannot be impersonal, lower than we make between ourselves. They must be at least personal. We might perhaps call them superpersonal, but my main answer to this question, and to the next, I find in the disclosure of Jesus. He is our surest guide in these matters.

The second question is: doesn't the size of the universe, shown by modern astronomy, mean that God must be so immense that, even if He is personal, personal relationships between Him and man are inconceivable? Quietly considered, that is not a difficulty, I think, for our reason, but only for our imagination. We let ourselves become mesmerized by astronomical figures. Then in effect we are asked, "How can you imagine that?" It adds up to trying to picture God as the chief executive of the universe, preoccupied with stars and nebulae, and with no time for the richness of human nature. Whatever God is, however, he is not that. The Bible and

29

contemporary theologians make that clear. What matters most is not size, whether Mount Everest or a giant star, but response, the human response of love. That is true for both you and for God, the real God, who is disclosed by and in Jesus.

Human love and loving God

If we are going on with this exploration, we must now inquire what kind of relationship we could have with God. Because He is unique, there can be nothing exactly like our relationship with God. There may well be resemblances, however, to our human relationships, because we remain in the same personalities, whether we are with God or with our friends. We are not Jekyll and Hyde.

Let us look then at human friendship and love. Always remember that there are many kinds. What I am about to say might apply to any real friendship, but for the sake of simplicity let us take the experience of marriage and see what light it may throw on our relationship with God.

The analogy is a well-known one. The Old and New Testaments use it. It seems to me a useful analogy, even though some of us may not be married or are unhappily married or have discovered our joy and fulfillment only in a second marriage. Like other priests, I see in my work all sorts of marriages at fairly close quarters, many joyful couples, some disappointed ones and some in sheer misery. To gain light on our relationship with God through a life of prayer, however, let us consider a marriage which, on the whole, is working out well. Of course, such a marriage cannot be put adequately into words, nor can the life of prayer. They are both too rich for that.

There is first the excitement of the wedding, reception, and honeymoon, of setting up home together in the first year or so. You may think you are an ideal couple, but living as close to one another as marriage requires, you are bound to have disagreements, perhaps sharp ones at times. You may

30

say, "I never thought this would happen with us." I suppose you should have known. It's sensible, though, isn't it, to say to one another you're sorry, even if it means sinking your pride, and to make it up each night before you go to sleep? If you don't, difficulties pile up. Then, saying you're sorry becomes more difficult. A wedge may develop between you. In some ways you may become strangers.

So it is with daily prayer. We need to watch, without being overanxious or too introspective, that no serious obstacles build up between God and us, or prayer, like some marriages, will become hollow and perhaps die.

Naturally the sparkle of the early stages of marriage is hardly likely to last forever. It may sometimes be for you like an exciting, blazing bonfire, but it can't always stay like that. I think, however, it should normally remain a good steady fire, and it often does, giving warmth to you and your family and many other people too.

Why doesn't that happen more often? Partly, I think, because the husband and wife take each other for granted. They don't appreciate each other as they used to. He says, "It's *only* the wife." She says, "It's *only* him." They lose interest in each other's hobbies. Birthdays and, worse still, anniversaries get forgotten. Signs of appreciation and tokens of affection day by day, morning and evening, fade away. These little tokens may not always express deep feeling, but they show there is caring, and to express love is often to increase love. They help to maintain the partnership of love that is being built up.

It is like that in the life of prayer. For many of us it is the *daily* coming to God, without much feeling sometimes, but always coming, seeking, appreciating, that in the long run builds up a life of fellowship in prayer. In his recent book on prayer, *The Christian Affirmation*, Father John Dalrymple calls prayer "a generative sign." Prayer is not only a sign of our love for God, it can often generate love within us. It can warm us up with a warmth that can spread to others. It can

31

help to humanize us. That is one reason why it is so vital to pray regularly.

As the years of married life go on, the husband may have increasing responsibilities in his work. He may be extremely busy and so quite probably is his wife. They still think of each other during the day, but not so much or so affectionately as they used to. Now there is not enough time to "talk" to each other and to be truly close. It may become difficult, when the relationship has worn thin like that, to patch up quarrels, to own up to being selfish.

With praying it is the same. "I do not need to stop for prayer; I'm busy," we say. "I pray at my work," or even, "I make my work my prayer." So easily said, and there is in fact something important in that. Prayer-at-work, however, will not be very deep prayer unless we also *make* times to be alone and quiet with God.

Men of prayer have made time for prayer. Few people have been busier than Jesus, caring for people, teaching them, forgiving them, healing them; yet he made time for quiet communion with God. He went out alone by Himself for prayer, early in the day and sometimes in the dead of night.

There is another similarity between love and prayer: Those deepest in love are, it seems to me, those who have been married longest. It is not quite the kind of love they began with, but it is a love so deep that by intuition each can now sense at once how the other is feeling, and knows how to meet that need. Together they have had all kinds of experiences, high moments, dull patches, times perhaps of total unresponsiveness, and more than once the question may have cropped up, "I wonder, have I made a mistake?" Somehow, though, by going through it all together, they have come to that deep knowledge of each other. That is real, generous love.

I am convinced that prayer is very similar. We shall only discover what real prayer is if we make up our minds to go on, through those times when it is so wonderful, through dull stretches of the journey, and through those hours when it all seems unreal. We shall then find for ourselves who God is and what is the richness of His love; this will give us love, joy and strength, which will in turn overflow to others. That is part of what it means to become truly human for their sakes.

For a moment, however, let us take an honest look at some difficult questions, and then continue our exploration.

"The evil in our lives is an obstacle to belief, and a thorn in the Christian's side." Austin Farrer, philosopher, theologian, poet and friend of mine for twenty-five years.

The problem of evil

Evil—suffering, cruelty, natural disasters—is the great obstacle to believing and prayer. It is no modern problem. Thinkers have faced it in all ages.

Someone has said, "This world is not much of a success as a pleasure garden, but then it was never *meant* to be one." The world is, rather, a place for person-building. While parents wish happiness for their children, they desire even more the development of their characters through personal relationships, and that development involves hard and painful effort. Presumably that is the divine purpose for us. It is also significant, according to Christian belief, that when the divine love entered the world so significantly in Jesus, that love encountered those evils, challenged them, and handled them. The struggle involved the cross, new power through Christ's resurrection, and leads on, so Christians are convinced, to a future triumph over evil.

Viewed in this perspective, although suffering still remains a massive evil, it has evoked from men and women amazing courage and love-in-action. Cruelty, too, remains evil, but perhaps cruelty is inevitable in human beings, who have free will, that free will which is essential if we are to know freely-given love, the most profound of human experiences. Natural disasters are indeed evils in the setting of self-conscious life. We live in a world which exhibits normal sequences of physical and chemical reactions, as, for example, the laws of gravity. The same sequences produce on the one hand showers, sunshine, and harvests, and on the other hand the threats of famine, earthquakes, and tidal waves. In a consistent universe, if may be that we cannot have one without the other. Furthermore, if life were arbitrarily cushioned too much—it sounds a hard thing to say—perhaps we should not become responsible, mature people, nor develop our talents. Man-come-of-age with his technological skills is challenged to foresee these dangers and to alleviate them, as far as possible.

All these evils are, I think, serious difficulties, but they are not impossible obstacles to belief. This must sound like cold comfort to many sufferers and especially to those who live among the hardships and injustices of the third world and I am far from satisfied with what I can write. Much more profound thought can be found in John Hick's *Evil and the God of Love* and Austin Farrer's *Love Almighty and Ills Unlimited.*

While we must not refuse to think about evil, our primary task is to fight against evil. We have to admit that we have an unsolved dilemma on our hands. So, however, if I understand it correctly, has the physicist. In his study of light he has to hold side by side two apparently different hypotheses, one an understanding light as wave motion and the other an understanding light as *quanta*, pellets of energy. The physicist's dilemma does not lead him to give up physics and take to painting instead. All fields of study have their unsolved problems. Even the graver problem of evil need not make the believer throw in the towel.

In the end we are faced by a choice, either to believe in God and accept this problem of evil, or to reject any belief in

God and somehow find an adequate explanation for the goodness in the world. Of these alternatives, I find the former less difficult, far less difficult, because of another, for me, very significant factor.

It is the following: There are times, I grant, when life is like a sky covered over with the black clouds of evil, suffering, cruelty, injustice, disasters, to say nothing of personal difficulties and frustrations. Yet, I am sure that at least one ray of light always pierces those clouds. That is enough to assure me that beyond the evil there is love. That ray is the person and life of Jesus Christ, who, I am convinced, discloses to us that which is at the heart of reality—God and His love. I would like to give my reasons for that conviction and then show its immense practical importance. First, however, let us remember that it is not only through Jesus that we receive light.

Men of faith

The New Testament makes it clear that from the beginning Christians have acknowledged that light comes to them from God, not just through Jesus but through other men as well. The letter to the Hebrews, for example, begins with this magnificent confidence: "God, who in many and varied ways spoke in times past to our forefathers through the prophets, has in these last days spoken to us by a Son." Or, to put it another way, the same God, who disclosed himself in a uniquely significant way in Christ, has also shown Himself to us through the prophets, those profound and fascinating Jewish men of faith and prayer: Amos, that farmer, who started a religious revolution; Hosea, who discovered the depths of God's love through loving his own wife when she was not true to him; those prophets who contributed to the great poetry of the Book of Isaiah; Jeremiah, whose soliloquies and protests awake echoes in our hearts, who longed for wife and family but kept himself free, *disponible*,* to serve

*available

37

his nation in its hour of crisis. In every age God has also spoken to us in the particular way needed through such men as Vincent de Paul, William Wilberforce or Martin Luther King, Jr. Furthermore, I find no difficulty in hearing God through the great men and women of other faiths. The New Testament itself says that Christ, the disclosure of God, enlightens *all* men, although they don't often recognize the source of their illumination. We rejoice at the immense spectrum of God's light among men.

The Man Jesus

It was, however, in quite an unparalleled way, I am convinced, that God has disclosed himself to us in Jesus. This makes the difference, not only as to how I face the problem of evil, but also as to how I hope to be able to live a truly human life today.

Although the divine broke through to us in an extraordinary way in Jesus, the first thing that impressed men about Jesus, and the first thing that still impresses us, is that He is more human, not less human, than we are. (I need not spend time here refuting the theory that Christ was a myth. His name appears not only in Christian writings, but also in the records of the Roman secular historians, Tacitus and Suetonius.) Jesus was man, flesh of our flesh. He was sensitive to the beauty of life and its tragedies. He knew hunger. Tiredness and exhaustion wore Him down. He cried at His friend's grave and over Jerusalem, the city he loved. He was a man of love. He loved Martha, Mary, and Lazarus. He loved his mother and there was a disciple whom he particularly loved. His heart warmed to a young man, rich and very "correct," who could not decide to join Him and His followers. Jesus had a sense of humor, he compared the unbending Pharisees with children who wouldn't join in the games of weddings and funerals.

Jesus needed to pray and sometimes He prayed with loud crying and tears. He was tempted, far more than we are tempted. We sometimes give in to temptation, for example, to excessive ambition, before temptation has reached its fullest intensity, but because Jesus went on resisting to the end, he felt temptation mounting to a pitch we have never experienced. He would not use divine power to make His life easier. He would not turn stones into bread to satisfy His hunger.

He knew what it was to be let down by friends. He felt deserted even by God. During His crucifixion He called out, "My God, my God, why have you forsaken me?" It seemed to Him that God was dead. In reality God was not dead, but that is how it felt to Jesus and may sometimes feel to us. God, because God is love, never deserts anyone.

Jesus was indeed man. Christians, through a mistaken reverence, have not always faced that fact. It has important implications for our life today. Jesus was not half-man, half-God. It is through the completeness of his humanity that the richness of the divine comes to us. Paul wrote, "In Christ the complete being of the Godhead dwells embodied." There are ample indications of full humanity in His life and teaching, in the gospels themselves. Not everything there is prosaically literal, but so much is "in character," that it all builds up to a consistent portrait.

The divine coming through in Jesus

We must face the preliminary question: "Do the gospels give us a reliable account of Jesus, particularly of His teaching?" The gospel writers could not carry out research as modern historians do, but they wished to write of Jesus as truly as they could. Luke explicitly said this at the beginning of his gospel. (We will look at this question in a little more detail later in this book.)

It was not only of Jesus as He was in Galilee that they wrote, it was also of the Jesus they knew in their prayer and daily living, the Jesus who shed light on the problems of their own day. That is true of all the gospels and particularly of St.

John's Gospel, yet C. H. Dodd, an outstanding New Testament scholar, has written:

> When all allowance has been made for these limiting factors—the chances of oral transmission, the effect of translation, the interests of teachers in making the "sayings" "contemporary" and simple human fallibilities—it remains that the first three gospels offer a body of sayings on the whole so consistent, so coherent, and withal so distinctive in manner, style and content, that no reasonable critic should doubt, whatever reservations he may have about individual sayings, that we find reflected here the thought of a single, unique teacher.

What did Jesus say? It would seem that He did not talk much about himself. He talked mostly about God and God's rule and love in the world. It is difficult to be quite certain what descriptive titles Jesus actually used about Himself, or people used about Him, or what their exact significance was. However, from words like these in both Matthew's and Luke's gospels, "No one knows who the Son is but the Father, or who the Father is but the Son, and those to whom the Son may choose to reveal him," it is clear that He had a relationship with God unparalleled even in the greatest men of any religion.

That comes out in many ways. Let me mention only one other instance. We read in the twelfth chapter of Mark the parable that Jesus told about the vineyard. The owner sent his servants to collect the grape harvest from the workers. The workers beat up the servants and sent them away with nothing. That happened more than once. Finally, the owner sent his son, saying, "They are bound to respect him." The workers murdered him, however, and flung his body out.

Jesus' message was clear both to his friends and to his opponents. The owner was God. The servants were the prophets: Amos, Hosea, Isaiah, Jeremiah, and the rest—the most inspired of men. When they were beaten and turned out, God said, "Then I will send not another prophet, but someone in quite a different category." Jesus was that someone. He had a unique relationship, an incomparable closeness to God. John's Gospel crystallizes this truth in the words, "Anyone who has seen me has seen the Father." That means that when we see Jesus and His unceasing love for people, we can say, "God is just like that." God has let us into the secret of what He Himself is.

Jesus' love is love-in-action, ready to help the widow who had lost her only son, ready to sit down to a meal with prostitutes and crooked tax collectors, caring for them as friends. Furthermore, His love is not a soft love. "Hypocrites, blind guides," Jesus called the Pharisees and ecclesiastical lawyers to their faces, not out of temper, but because he loved them. These strong words seemed to be the only way to set the Pharisees free from their hardness and legalism so they might love and serve others. This same strong perceptive love helped Jesus to sort out the problems of the woman at the well in Samaria and again his language was uncompromising.

All through His life we see that love, consistent, deep and strong, a love which is the disclosure of God, at the heart of reality in spite of all the evil in the world. That is the significance of Jesus for us today. That is central to our understanding of the whole of life. Norman Pittenger, a modern theologian, has summed it up, "Jesus Christ is the divine love itself, made man, and thus made available to us; this is utterly central."

Contemplative praying

The divine love is so central—and so humanizing. It is what I and many others in our present society need. The achievements of science are amazing, but so often our civilization seems to be out for efficiency and speed. It is pressuring us, hurrying us into treating men and women as types rather than persons, because we think we haven't time—or love—for more.

41

I do not know about you but I believe that if I am going to remain truly human, let alone Christian, I have somehow or other to open myself day by day to the warm, humanizing love which comes from God. That means prayer with a contemplative quality, a way of praying which is quite possible for ordinary people. (There are other ways of contemplative prayer, and I do not use "contemplation" in a technical sense.) For this kind of praying, words may not be very important. Rather, it is like being with a close friend, something too deep for words and often very refreshing. "Those who look to the Lord will win new strength." Any time in the day will do for this kind of prayer, but it needs to be frequent, and, if possible, daily. Prayer builds up like friendship and love. While the first thing in the morning is best for me, you may find quiet at some other time in a church, in a park, in a train, or even in an office, before others arrive or after they have left.

This kind of praying is not complicated. There are, I think, four elements in it, but they run into one another. It is similar to the way you contemplate something beautiful in nature or a work of art. You look at it leisurely, receptively, responsively, and, in a way, creatively, for your faculties are being heightened. Thus, you are changed a little and afterward see other things more sensitively.

First, then, in contemplative praying you need to be leisurely and to unwind. Some people, however, become so busy unwinding that they don't do much else. Perhaps all that is essential to remember is that God is at the heart of the reality we live in. He is our Lord, and He is as inseparable from us as the air we breathe.

Secondly, and much more important, we have to find out how to be receptive, how to receive that light, that love that pierces the clouds of life. There are so many ways, and we each have to discover our own to suit our varying circumstances. Perhaps we look at a crucifix, a picture, or icon and something of the divine love comes through to us. Sometimes, lines like these speak to us:

> My song is love unknown,
> My Saviour's love to me,
> Love to the loveless shown,
> That they might lovely be.

At other times to listen to music, to a recording, may bring the break in the clouds through which the light of God comes. At yet other times we remember moments in our lives when God's love has been specially disclosed to us. For some people the opening may come through recalling an experience of friendship which has been as wonderful as a sacrament, for human love can bring us divine love, as the bread and wine do in holy communion. Christians have always known that. Paul wrote to his friends in Philippi, "You know how I long for you all in the heart of Jesus Christ." The love they received from the apostle was a sacrament which brought to them also the love of God in Christ.

The recalling of friendship is close to the way which is perhaps for us, as Christians, the most frequently used of all, the way through the words of the Bible, not through random passages in the Bible, but through particular verses which almost unfailingly speak to our hearts and minds. Again, it is best for us to compile our own collections of verses. "God was in Christ reconciling the world to himself", "The Son of God who loved me and gave himself up for me", "All who are moved by the Spirit of God are sons of God" are a few examples I come back to again and again. Such passages become not only extracts from documents of a distant past, but also doors which can be pushed open quietly in the present moment and through which there shines the light and love which broke into the world in the life of Jesus. His love for Peter, for Nicodemus, for Zacchaeus, for everyone, comes to us.

43

Even if our prayer time has to be short, we must not feel hurried. We need to forget the ticking of the clock, to be deeply silent. That kind of receptiveness is the heart of contemplative praying.

Thirdly, we naturally wish to be responsive to God's love with our whole personality, as we like to respond to a friend. But we cannot always do that. Sometimes we are tired, or we feel "cold." Even then, however, we can respond with our minds, or at least we can make an effort to attend to the One who loves us. Thus, in some way we respond. God, so Jesus has disclosed to us, actually longs for our response and it brings him joy. The father in the parable ran down the road to welcome his son home and said, "Let's have a feast." Those words are, I grant, human and inevitably inadequate words, but they point to and stand for a reality—the joy we bring to God when we respond in prayer. So much does God desire our response that he pours his own love into our hearts through the Spirit. Human love is not strong enough. It needs enriching, deepening, directing. When we pray, it can be the Holy Spirit in His love, doing just that, working in us and gradually transforming us from inside. Deep down, we need to be quiet and remember His love.

Fourthly, contemplative praying is a creative experience. Afterward, our response should carry over creatively into our lives. "He who loves God loves his brother also." This is a sign that our response in prayer is authentic. We must not, however, get this wrong. There is the idea about in the world today that the only real way to love God is to serve our neighbor. Obviously it is not the only way. This idea is an understandable overcompensation from days when many praying Christians were often not ready to dirty their hands in the service of their neighbors. God longs for us to love all our neighbors, but He also longs for us to give our love directly to Him. A mother cares for her children and in this way expresses much of her love for her husband, but that is not the totality of a woman's love. There is the personal love

44

which her husband needs and which she is glad to give directly to him. So it is also with his love for her. All this is true of our love for God. Jesus invites us to love both God and our neighbor with our whole personality. God longs for our love, and He wishes to see the love, which unites us to Him, overflowing and spreading to all those who are round about us.

Our human love for one another can, we know, become possessive or even patronizing, or, if we do not soon see a response, hurt and discouraged. This is why our love for God is so important. Our love for Him should gradually remove those weaknesses from our human love.

When people begin to grow in love, they ask, "Is it for ever?"—a natural question and a right one. So it is in our growing love for God. His answer is, "Dwell, live, abide for ever in my love." We shall have our failures, but contemplative praying is open to us all and will help us. Through it the Spirit can transform us from inside and make us and keep us as human as Jesus.

I have experienced failure, as have we all. The most serious problem, however, is not failure itself, but being discouraged by failure, being turned in on ourselves in self-pity, and so being less open to others and to God. The tragedy of failure is that it may dehumanize us.

Jesus faced failure, but he was not dehumanized by it. The crowds who at first hung on his words faded away. Intimate friends deserted him. On Good Friday night the failure seemed to be complete.

Love and the passion of Jesus

Jesus had decided that He would do one thing, and nothing else. He did it: He loved, and did nothing else. He was never dehumanized. He said, "There's nothing else in life except loving God and those who come into your life with your whole being. Everything else turns on this." He said it and He lived it. Whether He was teaching or healing or fighting against evil, it was the love in His heart which was the motivating force.

His love evoked opposition, as love nearly always does. He challenged the legalists, who through their insistence on the letter of the law were going to stone a woman to death for adultery. Those men could not stand Jesus and His ways. They plotted. Jesus could see that it was going to mean death, but He went right on loving. He said He came, not to be served, but to love, to serve and to lay down His life "a ransom for many." He meant that through loving to the very end He would release into the world a new energy of love, powerful enough to set men and women free to meet, love and serve their neighbors. Jesus would not swerve from loving-to-the-end. In Gethsemane He was tempted to do so, but He would not; nor would He allow Peter to protect Him with his sword, so he went to execution. His terrible death was the climax of His loving. It was the hardest and the most wonderful thing He had to do, and He went right on, until finally He could say from the cross, "It is finished." The loving had been carried right through. That Good Friday night, however, was black. It seemed to be a stark failure.

Yet, on the next Sunday morning surprising things began to happen. Those friends who had come with Him from Galilee to Jerusalem and His disciples said, "We've experienced Him—again!" Jesus declared, "I am with you always, even unto the end of the world." He was, and is, with His friends with joy and love.

It is joy and love of that depth and quality which Jesus shows, that the world needs: our immediate neighbors, our country in its opportunities and tensions, the nations divided by fear and injustice, the third world. Wisdom, sacrifice and action are demanded, but to be effective they must spring from a love like Christ's, a love that understands, that strengthens and, when necessary, challenges. Some people have hardly tried to love, but many have tried, have been worn down, and failed. Failure in love is our most serious and basic failure.

Christ and ourselves

We are going to fail again and again unless we can find out how to live so close to Christ that His love and strength flow into us. Christ is the vine and we are, at least potentially, branches to bear fruit. The fruit is not merely individual

48

character, personal conduct. For the gospel does not say, "You shall bear fruit," but "You shall *go* and bear fruit." That fruit is our influence and action in the world. Only the steady flow of the sap from the vine can make the branches bear grapes. That is why we need to remain permanently close to Christ. "Abide in me and I in you, for apart from me you can do nothing."

In actual practice, how can we remain close to Christ, abide in Him? Clearly we can do so through prayer, particularly that receptive, contemplative praying we looked at in the last chapter. Human experience helps us to understand that. When we are close to someone, loving and loved, trusting and trusted, we may not need many words, but we are receptive and so we are strengthened to face the problems of life. It can be the same between the Lord and ourselves, but if it were only that, prayer might lead to mere passivity. We have to *live* in the world, close to Him, becoming assimilated to His outlook and character. That involves keeping our eyes open and making efforts. Only in that way can we abide in Him and go and bear fruit in the world. How do we set about this? We need to watch Jesus and then take a good look at ourselves.

First, we notice again how He cares for people and really meets them. He does not just brush shoulders with them. He sits down with them, He listens, He genuinely likes to be with them; He needs to feel their situation. Then He can understand and love. He sits with social riffraff and with cunning rogues. Equally, He sits with the "establishment" men, with the Pharisee who is very "correct," knows all the rules, and is a bit of a reactionary. He makes time for people. He may be tired, but not too tired to welcome the mothers and their children.

He is the same even when we might have expected Him to be overwhelmed with His own troubles. When He is dragging His cross in Jerusalem with all the horror of crucifixion before him, He turns to the women who have come to console him, and He is concerned not with His own, but with their troubles in the catastrophe to come. Finally, while in excruciating pain, He prays for the men just as they are crucifying him. This is love, ready at all times to go out to the needs of others.

What about ourselves, where we live, where we work, where the claims of nation and world meet us? True, we can't do everything. There just isn't time. Is lack of time, however, the only—or even the chief—reason why we don't do anything?

Secondly, we watch Jesus not only meeting others, but also knowing He has responsibilities for them. He takes a boat to go on holiday with His disciples. He enjoys himself with them, but He always remembers that He is training them for a task in the world. He puts up with their quarrels, He does not walk out on them. At times, His responsible love makes Him speak sternly to them. Jesus was not afraid of a row, when love demanded a row.

If we are trying to live close to Christ, we will see more clearly our responsibilities to those who employ us, to our colleagues, to those who depend on our work, to those we meet at parties and in our family circle. They have their problems and we have ours. The issues are often not sharply drawn, black or white. The only available solution is somewhere in between. Love forbids us to say, "It's all too complicated; I can't bother." It is for us to be sensitive to the Spirit of Jesus, to help others make responsible decisions, and become their best selves.

Thirdly, we see the immense courage of Jesus. When He had considered a matter, He was ready, if necessary, to take a bold, lonely line. That was not the hardness of a Stoic, for Jesus was a sensitive man. He felt it natural and right to depend on His friends. He spoke frankly of His needs to His disciples and longed for the support of their prayers. "My heart is ready to break with grief," He said in the garden of Gethsemane, "stop here, and stay awake."

50

We, too, should realize our dependence on one another and our need of the love and prayers of others. Having said that, however, we know that sometimes, like Jesus, we need the courage to take a lonely line, but a lonely line inspired by love.

Fourthly, Jesus was a man with great gifts. He developed and used them with wisdom and love for the true good of others. He was not a man to bury His talents in the ground. He didn't lack the courage and the energy to develop His gifts. He had clarity of mind and facility of speech, he could go right to the point. He had to learn how. His feelings were rich and deep. He had his moments of tears, He did not mind people seeing them, and His moments of joy. He loved His friends, and His kind of loving brought them new hope, new strength, new *élan*.

What is happening to our gifts? Are our minds becoming better informed and better used in the service of our neighbors? Does our love bring joy, richness, and resilience to others? There is an element of adventure and risk in the constructive use of all our gifts. It is disastrous to bury them for safety.

A fifth attribute of Jesus strikes me—and this may be a reason why He worked everything out so well: He was a man of genuine worship and prayer. He used to go regularly to the worship in the synagogues. They were often dull places and some of the rabbis were very dull men, but still Jesus went. Odd as it may seem to some of us, He used to go to the Temple where animals were still sacrificed. Jesus would do nothing against his conscience but, short of that, He went along with everybody. He never let himself feel "superior." He entered into the common life and the common worship. He knew others needed that bond, and so did He. He was a man of personal prayer. Before it was light, and apparently after an exhausting day, He was up and out in a lonely spot for prayer. After teacher and feeding the crowds, He climbed the mountainside by the lake in the stillness of the evening.

He was hungry, as we should be, for solitude, to be alone with God.

Repentance

If we wish to bring understanding love to others, we must face the facts about the differences between Jesus and ourselves. We may feel like putting this off. We may be afraid that it will serve only to increase our present sense of failure. The object of facing our faults, however, is to reduce our feeling of discouragement. We are not expected to achieve perfection. We are asked to look at Jesus Christ and to let Him, by his Spirit, draw us nearer to Himself—that's all. That involves praying and being open to the Spirit of God, so that He can help us to do four things: see the facts about ourselves; acknowledge our failures; have that freedom which comes with forgiveness; take positive action about the future.

First, we need God's help to face the facts about ourselves in the light of Christ. To do so is one of the marks of being human. An unexamined life is an inhuman life. No excessive, unhealthy introspection is called for just a side glance at ourselves as we think about Jesus in the New Testament. We need a checkup as we prepare to receive Him in Holy Communion, and from time to time, perhaps before Christmas and Easter, we need a more thorough overhaul.

Secondly, we should own up to God about our failures. While they may not disrupt our relationship with Christ, the True Vine, we must recognize them for what they are. We may need also to apologize for our faults to people we may have hurt, sometimes unintentionally, sometimes quite intentionally. We must be careful not to cause further pain by the way we apologize; still less must we reopen old wounds.

Thirdly, we need to be sure we are forgiven, then we shall not be discouraged by a sense of failure. God, as Jesus has made clear, desires to forgive us more than we wish to be forgiven, but no friend can give us a present unless we open our hands to receive it. Often, our trouble is that we do not open our hands to receive God's gift of forgiveness because of an unhappy, misguided sense of self-sufficiency, or even through a simple lack of courage.

He is waiting to say to us, "Your faults are forgiven; go in peace." "Christ died for us while we were yet sinners, and that is God's own proof of his love towards us." God doesn't say, "Try to reform yourself, and afterward I'll reinstate you." We may think that this unqualified forgiveness is imprudent and rash, but it is not that God or we acquiesce in our faults. Rather, out of deep gratitude for what God has already done for us in forgiving us freely, we collaborate with Him in letting Him make us what He wants us to be. That is God's way, His way of making us humbly and truly human.

For the method to be effective, we must have the certainty that our faults are really forgiven. That certainty God Himself conveys to the hearts of some people inwardly and directly; others need to hear the words of forgiveness spoken. The Jewish woman, who wept for her faults at the feet of Jesus in the Pharisee's house, could presumably have known from the Psalms that God would forgive her as soon as she turned to Him, but she needed to hear for herself the words, "Your sins are forgiven." There were many in our Lord's lifetime who needed to hear these words said, and there are many still today. "Confess your sins to one another." It was, I think, to meet that continuing need that, according to Chapter 20 of St. John's Gospel, the Risen Christ gathered round Him His disciples and told them that they could now continue to do what He had been doing, assuring men and women of God's forgiveness. "Receive the Holy Spirit. If you forgive any man's sins, they are forgiven; if you pronounce them unforgiven, unforgiven they remain." It looks to me as if the Lord expected people to come at times one by one to the apostles, and I should think that the apostles were normally able to say, "Yes, your sins are forgiven." Only if there was some obvious insincerity would an apostle have to say, "No, for the moment I cannot assure you of forgiveness."

Also, it seems to me that all this refers to the faults of individuals, not to a congregation of people making a general confession together.

All down the centuries, and in various ways, people have gone to their ministers, not, of course, for their ministers to forgive them, but to receive through their ministers the assurance that God has indeed forgiven them. This has clearly been the case in the Eastern Orthodox Churches, in the Roman Catholic Church, and to a lesser extent in the Anglican and other Churches. It is probably being used more now in the Reformed Churches, largely through the influence of the Taizé community.

This path to forgiveness has been misused. It is for us to consider whether a wise use of it might not help to make us more deeply human and more able to bring love to others. The prejudices against confession seem largely to have evaporated, perhaps because people are in general more open with one another than they used to be, to say nothing about how much they are willing to tell psychiatrists! While I can understand some having hesitations, all I can say is that confession has been of enormous help to me and, as far as I can see in my work, a great help to many others.

The motives that bring people to confession are varied. Some come because they think it is one of the best ways to receive advice. They know that the priest will give no secrets away, so they feel able to put all their cards on the table. Others come to be set free from their sense of discouragement. Perhaps some say, "I can never forgive myself for some things I have done." Then they discover that God himself has forgiven them and they can see life in a new perspective. Others say, "Confession is the way for me, if I am going to deal with my faults realistically. That is the way to deal with my self-sufficiency and pride; it will make me more humble, more objective, more human. It has helped many others to live nearer to God, and it may well help me."

It is not too difficult to do, though it may call for some

courage. We need first to find a priest who has had some training and experience in such matters and arrange a preliminary talk with him. He will not be shocked at whatever we may have to say. That is his job, like the physician in his examining room. We need not say, "I shall never be able to face him again after this." I have never found any embarrassment of that kind. The priest who heard my first confession—and it was a difficult confession—remained one of my closest friends. Nor should we ever say, "It's no good my confessing that, because I might do it again." Of course we might, but it is better to go and apologize, even if we slip again, than to be too proud to apologize at all.

Confession may be made in church or in more informal ways. It is not only for those who are interested in religious affairs. Years ago I had been speaking about it in a London church where I was giving a course. I happened to be in the church the next morning when quite an old man, not particularly well educated or at all religious, came up to me. From his first words I thought he had been annoyed by the previous evening's address, but not at all. We talked things over. Then I sat and waited for a few minutes. He hobbled up the church and confessed all he could remember of his life in fairly blunt language. I assured him of God's forgiveness. I have never seen an old man's face change in such a remarkable way. He had received the peace that passes all understanding.

This may not be the best way for everyone, but we all need to face the facts about ourselves, to be no longer discouraged by our failures, to live closer to Christ. Then we can bring His love and joy to those round about us, to the world in its need.

Forgiveness matters, but it is only half of what matters; the other half is facing the future with a sense of freedom.

5   "YES" TO GOD WITH JOY

As we look towards the future, it would be interesting to compare notes on what we think a Christian is. We should first reflect about genuine Christians we've met or read about. Our answer would also have to stand the test of common sense, and it would have to be related to life as it is today.

"A Christian," I would say for a start, "is someone who says 'Yes' to God—and tries to say it with joy."

Isn't it often like that when we begin, or start a new stage in, the Christian life? Something we have heard, or read, or something that has happened, makes an impression on us. Or, we've looked honestly at life, as we are trying to do in this book, at what men and women can become, and particularly at Jesus himself, and we notice, I think, pointers to something transcending our own past experience. There are still concepts we are not clear about, but we feel we can say: "Yes, I'll explore a little further," or "Yes, I'll respond to what seems to draw me on." It is "Yes" after "Yes," with plenty of reflection in between as we go ahead unblinkered— and joy, believe me, comes. We don't always feel we're at top form, yet the New Testament talks about our Lord putting his own joy into our hearts. We begin to understand this. It is something like the joy that comes to us in a growing friendship as we feel ourselves more and more understood, loved and trusted.

Moreover, doesn't the experience of human love and trust help us to understand it? "Yes," we say to a friend, "let's meet." We talk, we argue, and then we say, "Yes, we'll do that together." Being together, reflecting, discussing, finding joy together lead us on from one "Yes" to the next. If this relationship should lead to marriage, each says at the wedding, "Yes, I'll trust myself to you." In that partnership there will be much to talk over and to do together. There will perhaps be times of disagreement and tensions, yet underneath you keep on saying, or feeling, your "Yes" to one another day by day. That is how, isn't it, you come to understand one another, have confidence in one another, and discover and explore the depths and richness of being truly human?

Your joy both in loving and being loved enriches others. If you hugged it all to yourselves it might easily fade away. We do not say "Yes" to God just to have a warm personal relationship with him for ourselves. To say "Yes" to God is to say "Yes" to life, to people, to society. We say "Yes" to God by doing the tasks of daily life and not putting things off. We say "Yes" to Him by meeting people and not dodging their real needs. We say "Yes" to Him by looking society in the face, rejoicing in its true achievements and fighting against its evils.

We began by glancing at Teilhard de Chardin, a man who brought much depth of understanding to others out of his own courageous exploration of life. He wrote of his own decision to take "great care never to stifle or distort or waste my own power to love and to do." His words may help us as we try to say "Yes" to God through and in the events of life.

You may say that is a tall order. Where does the strength come from, the power to love and to do, with joy? I would say—and you will see that I am basically a practical person— through Jesus ever-present with us.

We know we can receive power from others. Strength and confidence pass into us when, in the high mountains, we are roped to an experienced guide—he knows where the going is rough, he knows in detail the glaciers, he knows at once what to do in an emergency. When in ordinary life, we are under stress we can receive much strength from a true friend, one who has had perhaps a wider and deeper experience of life. Something of him passes into us. This can be so also, I am certain, when we are close to our Lord, not the Jesus of past history, but the risen and ever-present Lord. His strength becomes ours, through love.

Such has been the experience of great Christians. Paul the Apostle went through life saying his "Yes" to God in the power which came to him through his love of the Risen Jesus. That is how he managed in his lifetime to transform what looked like a small narrow sect among the Jews into a Church known throughout most of the civilized world, a Church of freedom, love, and joy. He succeeded because he was—I can use no other word—a passionate lover of Jesus, and he did not care who knew it. Of course Paul had his blind spots—so has everyone else. His letters show us his frustrations, his tears, and his joys. He was a richly human man. He says, "To me to live is Christ," as a man might say of his beloved, "She's everything to me, she's my life." Again he writes, "I live; yet no longer I, but Christ lives in me. And the life which I now live in the flesh, in the hard everyday circumstances of life, I live in faith in the Son of God. I live the great 'Yes' I am always saying to the Son of God who loved me and gave himself up for me."

That is what a Christian is. You and I are invited to explore the same country. The apostle may be a long way ahead of us, more loving, more generous, more courageous, but it is the same route for us. We keep our eyes wide open, we make time to reflect, we say "Yes" to God again and again with joy in the power of the Risen Christ, the Christ of the present moment.

The Risen Christ

What is the practical importance then for us of Christ's Resurrection? It is not only that we should like to know what happened to Jesus' dead body. No, it is something far deeper, something which touches the basic motivation of our lives and our resources for loving.

We are invited to make the motive behind our work and life, as it was for Jesus, the desire to help people become more truly human through our loving them. Many people, including some agnostics, do that, and often heroically, in a universe which they regard as "cold" or even hostile to their efforts, and they do it sometimes with a determination which is rather grim. We should be able to do it with at least an equal perseverance but with confidence and gaiety, because we are convinced as Christians that at the heart of all human life is God who is love. It is the Resurrection of Christ which makes us able to affirm that God is love and so to say, with joy, "Yes" to God in life.

Let my try to explain. Affirmation of God is clearly basic to Christianity. It is expressed in John's Gospel when he says that anyone who has seen Christ has seen the Father. That means, as we have noticed before, that whenever we look at Jesus, we have God's immense love-in-action shown to us and brought to us. That affirmation is also what lies behind all that Jesus said about Himself and His unique relationship as Son to the Father.

Suppose, however, He was mistaken. On Good Friday night it seemed as if He had been mistaken. He was dead and hurriedly buried. It looked as though it was all over. Then, starting on Easter day, a series of strange things began to happen. "God has raised Him to life again," the disciples declared, as they interpreted those happenings. "God has made this Jesus, whom you crucified, both Lord and Christ." If this statement is really true, then its significance for us is clear.

It is as if Jesus' life of caring and his fundamental message that God is love were written on a document. Then, by raising Jesus from the dead, God has, as it were, stamped the document with his great seal. He has ratified it and declared, "This is utterly true."

60

Did it really happen? Did the disciples get it right? There is no overwhelming demonstration of Christ's resurrection, from the nature of the case there could not be. However, there are at least three indications, to me convincing: the early Christian community with its courage and love, the evidence for the empty tomb, and those who said they had seen the Lord again. Not everyone will find each of these three indications equally impressive, but at least there is a variety of clues which invite us to explore further.

The first indication is the courage of the early Christians when they spoke of their conviction that Christ was risen, and the love which grew out of that conviction.

On the night before Good Friday, Judas betrayed Jesus, Peter denied him and the other apostles fled. Then, suddenly, on Easter day the disciples were convinced that they had again met Jesus alive, and soon they were speaking in the streets and in the judicial courts of his resurrection. They faced violence, prison and death for their conviction. How can we account for the change in them, except through the truth of their words?

Perhaps we may mention Paul again. In a letter to the Corinthians he claims to have seen the Risen Lord at his conversion on the road to Damascus, just as the others had met him at Easter time. How can we explain his *volte-face*? How was he changed from the violent persecutor of the first Christians into Paul, the missionary, whose life was packed with labors and dangers in the service of Jesus, the Lord whose resurrection was the focus of His gospel? "If Christ was not raised, then is our gospel null and void," he wrote, "and so is your faith, and we turn out to be lying witnesses for God."

The Christians spread to Rome and met, with the same courage, the Emperor Nero's persecution. The same audacity has appeared again and again down through the centuries and produced a movement which, indisputably, has altered world history.

What happened at Easter sparked off not only a new

courage, but also a new love for their Lord and for their neighbor. It was a love deep enough to impel the first Christians to pool all their goods, to live together with a new spontaneity and joy, attracting others to their Lord. Of course there were failures and relapses, but the young Christian communities springing up at surprising places around the Mediterranean brought new courage, new joy, new love to the world. They were convinced—and we should give serious consideration to their words—that the courage and love was not their own, but came to them from the Risen Lord. They were living "in the power of His resurrection."

That is the first of our indications; Christians can add to it today. Indeed, if some of those who are at present without Christian faith are ever going to believe, it will not be initially through their reading the gospels and examining the evidence for Christ's resurrection. It will be rather because they see first in the Christian community and in our lives a quality of love-in-action which they do not see anywhere else and which makes them ask, "Where does it come from?" Indications have to be seen.

As for the evidence for the empty tomb, let me make two preliminary statements. First, the gospels make it clear that Jesus' body was not merely resuscitated, reanimated, but rather was raised and in some way transformed. That is the reason why the Risen Christ was often not recognized at first sight and why he could appear and disappear in surprising ways. Christians have sometimes depicted the resurrection in too naive a way. Secondly, in my personal opinion, a miraculous explanation of the empty tomb, like other miracles, would not *a priori* be absolutely ruled out by the scientific laws of nature. Those so-called laws are not, if I understand them correctly, inflexible regulations of a closed system of nature, but rather they are only the shorthand summaries of a very large number of experiments and observations. If you ask a scientist, "Can miracles happen?" He can only reply, I feel, if he confines himself to his own field of study, "That is a question I am not competent to answer. The most I can say is that we do not happen to have miracles in our scientific records." You and I, therefore, can examine the evidence for the empty tomb for ourselves with an open mind.

Then what about it? How large a gap of time is there between the event and our first evidence? Our earliest record is in 1 Corinthians 15, written twenty years after the event, though Paul may be quoting from a tradition which he received at the time of his conversion ten or fifteen years earlier. That record does not state that the tomb was empty, but it implies it. The next witness, Mark's Gospel, written thirty years after the event, says that the tomb was empty, as do the other gospels, which were written from forty to seventy years after the happening.

My own considered opinion is that the tomb was empty because the body had been raised and transformed. How else could it be empty? I do not find satisfactory the other suggested explanations. I cannot think that a wild beast broke into the tomb and dragged the body away, or that the women and the apostles found an empty tomb because they went to the wrong tomb, nor can I believe that a group of Jews stole the body, mutilated or concealed it somewhere, and then allowed the apostles to get away with their assertion that the Lord has risen from the tomb. The suggestion that the apostles took away the body, hid it, declared that Christ was risen, and were ready to suffer repeatedly and gladly for this claim, knowing that it was a hoax, would seem to me psychologically impossible.

The third indication is the claim of those who said that they had met Jesus again. Incidentally, at this point it is worth noticing that what convinced Mary Magdalen that Christ was risen was not the empty tomb—that only left her crying in despair—it was when he met her. It was then that it came home to her.

What can we say honestly about those who claimed that they had met Jesus again? The first were Mary Magdalen and her companions, naturally overwrought, in the garden in the dim light of dawn. We might be rather dubious about the resurrection if their evidence stood alone, but it does not. Later that day and during the next few weeks many others claimed to have met him. All of them were, it is true, already his followers, yet they were at first skeptical of all reports, and the last experience it seems any of them expected was to see Christ alive again. Paul adds significantly to our information. He tells of one occasion when over five hundred Christians met the Risen Lord, most of them still alive and able to be questioned. Those meetings with the Risen Jesus do not look like "wishful thinking." I think this evidence is impressive.

Those indications are only indications. They will not compel anyone to believe. They suggest, I think, directions for exploration. If we are to find the Risen Christ, however, we need times for honest reflection, times to pray. We shall need to care for men and women in the way that Jesus cared for them. Sometimes, when we are caring for others in this spirit the hints, which have come to us in reflection and prayer, "click together," and we are convinced. That is part of the search. I had this in mind when we began this book with the four needs of mankind.

John Masefield at the end of his play, *The Trial of Jesus*, has Pilate's wife, on Good Friday evening, ask the centurion who watched the crucifixion, "Do you think Jesus is dead?"

"No, Lady," he responded, "I don't." "Then, where is he?" "Let loose," he replied, "in *all* the world, Lady, where neither Roman nor Jew can stop his truth."

Christ in the life of today

Where then can we meet with the Lord today? Where can we say "Yes" to him?

We can do so in innumerable places and ways, for Christ comes to us, both in the events of daily life and in the silence of our reflection and prayer. Francis of Assisi said "Yes" to our Lord in the road when he leaped off his horse and kissed the leper. He also said "Yes" to the Lord when in the silence of his heart he heard the words of the gospel, "Go, preach that the kingdom of heaven is at hand," and penniless he went and did it. We have records of this call and response in the lives of many Christians, and I think these moments come, and come repeatedly, into many people's lives. Like other deeply personal moments, they are seldom talked about. They are too precious for that.

The experience of Christ came, I believe, to John, the author of the Apocalypse. He was a pastor in Asia Minor, expelled by the government to Patmos, a lonely island for political prisoners. There, he had so profound an awareness of the Risen Lord that he fell to the ground like a man dead. He couldn't describe what had happened. His words can't be taken literally, but his first chapter, that bizarre mass of poetic images, all redolent of the Old Testament, conveys to us something of the reality and the wonder of the Risen Lord. Christ's constant presence with his people and His unchanging love for them were impressed indelibly upon John's consciousness in the Lord's words, "I am the first and the last, and I am the living one; for I was dead and now I am alive for evermore." That gave John a deep conviction that he must write to the Christians in his care in the seven cities of Asia Minor. He felt inwardly that he must help them share in some degree his own experience of the Risen Christ. For it was that which would enable them to face up to their threatening dangers: persecution, the infiltration of false teaching, and a subtle accommodation to worldly standards.

In his letter to the Christians at Laodicea, John told them that the Risen Christ was standing and knocking at their door. It was not a knock to be feared, like the knock of the secret police in the night. It was the knock of a friend, inviting them to the joy of a feast. If they could say their "Yes" to the Lord, they would receive from him the courage and love they needed to face the pressures of their Christian life.

Moments of choice happen more often than we realize.

The ever-present Risen Christ knocks at the door of our lives, but often we do not notice who is there. His knock may come in the jolt we feel at some unexpected piece of news, in something said by a friend or by a critic, in something which strikes us as we are reading, in something which pops up into our consciousness in a time of reflection. We turn away so easily and go back to our normal routine. We are afraid of what might disrupt the present pattern of our lives. We forget that invitations to move on and to change are often the Lord's way with us.

Our analogy of pointers, indications, and a route ahead is no more than an aid to thought. We must not press the analogy too far. The Christian life is a search, a reaching out to God. Even more, it is an opening of ourselves to the God who has now already come to the door of our everyday lives.

The heart of the Christian life is our saying "Yes" to Him. Unfortunately, it is possible to be involved in Christian activities for years without coming to the heart of the matter. High moral standards, regular prayer, and worship clearly have never been enough (though many may think so) for too easily do those activities become routine and self-satisfying. We can talk a lot about God without saying "Yes" to God. Jesus knew many people like that. Their hearts were closed. He told them, "I never knew you," although they said that they had spoken in His name.

We need to go on saying this "Yes" over wider and wider areas of our lives and with increasing depth. Paul, although he had said a decisive "Yes" to Christ on his road to Damascus, admitted in a letter years later that he still had a long way to go to complete his "Yes." He was straining forward like an athlete, he said, and still pressing on.

Whenever in our daily life we hear the tap of the Lord's invitation, we should try to turn to Him with heart and mind. Perhaps He is asking if He may come farther into our lives, bringing his *own* love and power so that we may be able to understand and love more effectively that particular person, or ourselves enter into a deeper relationship with Him, the

True Vine. We must be precise, life is not to be an unending series of New Year's resolutions, yet vagueness can be an undetected snare. I find it important to jot things down in black and white, but unfortunately I often make the mistake of thinking that to write a thing down is the same as doing it!

We must be practical. New capacities, old capacities at a new depth, a responsiveness to something so inner that we did not know it was there before—these must be practised. A little more courage is sometimes what we need. Jesus' own contagious courage will help us to give the door a pull. His joy will oil its rusty hinges: "that my joy may be in you." In our hearts we know by now He will understand, love, and accept us and our needs.

It may give us a little more staying power, if we tell a friend what we are planning. Our true strength of course will come from the Lord, who rose again to pour into us His grace, His own strength. We must not be discouraged about possible future failure. Even if we fail, that really won't matter so much, providing failure doesn't make us despair, but rather makes us turn at once to the Lord and rely more on him.

It was the Lord himself who said, "My grace is all you need; power comes to its full strength in weakness." He said it to Paul. And out of his own experience Paul answered, "When I am weak, then am I strong." That is the man who so steadily, so humanly, so effectively said "Yes" to God with joy in the power of the Risen Christ.

6   THE CHURCH AND THE IMPACT
OF THE RISEN CHRIST

An avalanche of invective fell on us. Some of it was exaggerated, as it always is, but much of it stuck. A thousand representatives from the churches all over the world were crammed into the auditorium of the Swedish university at Uppsala. The speaker was an ex-Christian minister, the black American novelist, James Baldwin, the son of a store-front Harlem preacher. He let us have it: all the injustices and the life-denying narrowness of the churches. "I wonder," he ended, "if there is left in the Christian churches the moral energy, the spiritual daring, to atone, to repent, to be born again."

"What can *we* do about it?" you may ask. Well, daring to be born again involves saying "Yes" to God, responding to his love—and getting on with it. We cannot do this only as individuals, however, we need to do it with others as the Church.

Many people, even some Christians, understandably, have no use for the Church, or at least not for the Church as it has been and as they see it now. But what really is the Church? It is not what many people think it is. Perhaps we should take a fresh look at it.

At heart, the Church is a company of people in all lands who wish to say a joyful "Yes" to God, to be open and human, to experience the impact of the Spirit of the Risen

Lord and the love he has brought into the world, and to transmit the impact of that love with mounting reverberations to all men.

The humanness of the first churches

Jesus thought a Church was needed and he trained the disciples. We watch Paul founding churches—and what churches! They were not "ideal" churches, they had plenty of warts. They are not, moreover, the blueprints for our churches; they belong socially to an age that is dead and gone. They were, however, churches alive with love, started by men on fire with a love for the Risen Jesus and for their fellow men. Look again at Paul. His love was no placid love, neither for Jesus nor for his friends. When he had disturbing news of his friends, he couldn't rest. He had to send off, posthaste, the only companion he had with him to find out what was happening. Back that companion came with good news and Paul wrote with joyful relief, "It is the breath of life to us that you stand firm in the Lord." To another group he had to send the kind of severe letter he didn't like writing, but to avoid misunderstanding he felt he must write again, and so he added, "That letter I sent you came out of great distress and anxiety; how many tears I shed as I wrote it! But I never meant to cause you pain. I wanted you rather to know the love, the more-than-ordinary love, that I have for you." That very love also made him strike out sometimes against those who were disrupting the little communities. He called such men dogs and sham-apostles. He hated himself for writing like this, but he felt he must. "I wish I could be with you now; then I could modify my tone; as it is, I am at my wits' end about you."

It was his love which brought those distresses on him. Love has never been a primrose path; love may involve a sharing of distresses and burdens, but love generates the energy and courage to share them. With Paul joy was always breaking through. Even in prison he wrote to his friends, "Rejoice in the Lord always; again I say, Rejoice." It is joy in the Lord, the joy that springs from union with the Lord, just as joy wells up from human love. So he transmitted to others the impact of the love of the Risen Lord.

Who were the friends he wrote to, who met in one another's houses: the family of Aristobulus, the household of Narcissus, Aquila and Prisca and the "church in their house"? They are mere names to us, but they were not mere names to Paul. There was Philemon with his wife Apphia, to whom he sent from prison a charming letter with the postscript, "Have a room ready for me, for I hope that, in answer to your prayers, God will grant me to you." What kind of people were they? A few were able, very able, like Apollos, the learned convert from Judaism, and Paul himself. Most of them, however, were slaves. Few had much education. Very few came from families of any social standing. Many of them, at least in the past, would have been in trouble with the police, if there had been police in those days.

Even now as Christians they would have serious failings. They were too attached to their favorite leaders: Paul, Peter, or Apollos. They formed cliques. Some took too much to drink even at meetings for worship. They had marital and sexual problems and wrote to the apostle about them. They were worried also about those who had died. They were, in fact, a very mixed bunch of ordinary people. God could, and still does, work through such people.

How Paul regarded the Church

And Paul called the early followers of Jesus the Bride of Christ and the Body of Christ. Neither these nor any other words are adequate to describe their relationship, and our relationship, to Christ. It is too complex, too rich. These two phrases, however, illuminate profound aspects of our union with Christ, even while we are still struggling with our faults, doubts, and inadequacies.

The Bride of Christ—no better words could be found to

71

express the closeness of Christians to their Risen Lord. Paul and other New Testament writers used it to speak primarily of the dependence of the whole Church on Christ and of its loyalty to Him. This magnificent phrase will have no substance, no reality, however, unless Christians know the one-to-oneness of their own relation to him. As His bride we Christians give our love to Christ and realize our glad dependence, a mature, adult dependence, on Him. We discover that it is in union with Him that we can go and bear fruit in our service in the world, through our union with Him we can come to a deeper communion with one another.

The other great metaphor Paul used is the Body of Christ. God works, of course, in the world outside the Church through secular men and secular agencies. We Christians must see how best we can work with them, but it is especially through small communities of believers, like those Paul cared for so deeply, that God wishes to prolong that impact of love which Christ brought into the world. What in practice did that mean for them and what does it mean for us? We must feel that Christ needs us. He needs us in all our rich variety. No one is to feel unimportant, left out. A quiet unassuming Christian may be as vital to the Body of Christ as an artery hidden in our physical bodies. Our gifts and our humanness are to be developed in his service. A Christian does not leave gifts buried and unused, through nervousness or lack of initiative. What is most important is that we should all realize that we depend on one another. If one of us is in distress, we should all feel it as members of the one Body. (If a virus really gets into your body, you feel it all over.) On the other hand, if one member is glad, we all should share his gladness. For that to happen we have to discover how to give ourselves in love to Christ and to one another in the one Body.

In these ways, we form the Bride of Christ and the Body of Christ, to transmit the impact of His love to the world of our day. The New Testament itself says that in the life of Jesus we see only what He began to do and teach. He longs to continue it through us. This does not mean a superficial copying of his methods in our twentieth century. The heart of His life must be the heart of our life.

Christ and his Church

Before we look at the Church today, let us glance at a few characteristics of our Lord's own life which should clearly mark the life of His Church.

Love, as we have seen, was the motive of all He did. When His Church serves, teaches, or challenges evil, a love like His should be its driving energy.

Teaching the gospel is an indispensable part of the Church's work, although stress is now placed rightly on service and identification with others. Jesus, we remember, was called Rabbi—teacher. How He spoke!—with words that went to the heart, with sparkling parables straight from life and with questions like, "What do *you* think?" We, the members of His body, must be trained to know what to say and how and when. We can't dodge that responsibility.

Christ's eyes were set on humanity and He looked into the future, although His working years were short and confined to a small country. The master passion of His life was the coming of God's kingdom. That is wider than nation or church; it is all humanity receiving and responding to the revealing love of God. "Thy kingdom come." Jesus and the New Testament writers painted its climax in dramatic colors. Paul wrote of it as "the universe, all in heaven and in earth, brought into a unity in Christ." Words, once more, are trying to do what words cannot do, but they point to a consummation, whose full reality lies beyond history, in a life to come, when "the splendor of the nations shall be brought into it." The Church needs to keep her eyes open to this splendor, which is no dream or wishful thinking, as our next chapter will make clear.

Universality of vision marks the parting command of the Risen Lord to the disciples: Go from Jerusalem "to the ends of the earth." Just before that command came the seminal words, "You will receive power when the Holy Spirit comes upon you." The early Christians meditated on all the Lord's words about the Spirit. Thus they could claim eventually—in words never to be forgotten—to walk in the Spirit, pray in the Spirit, rejoice in the Spirit, be strong in the Spirit.

This is close to what is perhaps the most striking mark of the life of Jesus Himself, noted by all students of the gospels: His sense of entire dependence upon and intimacy with the Father. Rudolf Bultmann remarks that, for Jesus, God is "*a God at hand.*" Joachim Jeremias, after a minute examination of Jewish and early Christian documents, has shown that when Jesus spoke to God as *Abba*, his native Aramaic word expressing affectionate trust in a father, "it was something new, something unique and unheard of." Further, He invited His followers in using this word, *Abba*, "to participate in His own communication with God." C. H. Dodd also has written of Jesus' sense of intimacy with His Father (though it was temporarily clouded over, even for him, in Gethsemane and on the cross): "Here is to be found the driving force and source of energy for an almost impossible mission, here certainly the source of the inflexible resolution with which he went, knowingly, to death in the service of his mission." The same source of energy is available to us, we may be sure, as we continue, in the Spirit, Christ's work for the kingdom of God.

Our tasks today

What does all that add up to? How do we transmit the impact of the Risen Christ to our world today? The ways are innumerable. We need to discover them ourselves: by reflecting, by prayer, by talking them over together and by taking action. As an invitation to further exploration, I should like to jot down a few ideas which occur to me.

First, the Church needs to be—and needs to be seen to be—outwardgoing, efficiently helping men and women to become fully human. The Church should, I think, be concerned with its internal affairs only sufficiently to keep Christians alert, informed, and vital. Their eyes should be on

for different types of people are necessary to complement one another. Paul said that it is only in the company of "all God's people" that we can come to grasp what is "the breadth and length and height and depth of the love of Christ."

Such congregations will need to maintain church buildings. The silent church building is a near necessity for those who live in crowded houses or busy hostels, an oasis in the modern urban desert of noise. There, busy people can begin to discover what it is to wait contemplatively on God, and what deep consequences that may have for our service in the world as the Body of the Risen Christ.

Some churches will always, I hope, be able to have worship on a large enough scale so that an inquirer or a worshiper can slip in and out anonymously, and not be given an effusive welcome and invited to join this or that group. There have been stages in my life when I have wished to be an anonymous seeker. If this hadn't been a possibility, I might have become a complete "drop-out" from the Christian faith.

Later, I wanted only a one-to-one contact with the Church, a discussion with a Christian friend. Only much later was I ready for the fellowship of a small group. For some Christians, that stage may just possibly not come at all. We need to be very flexible. Not all relations between Christians can be the close I-thou kind; the less committed I-you relations are quite legitimate, and indeed to try to eliminate them in the Church might lead to disaster—or to hypocrisy.

Fifthly, and most important of all, the Lord cannot use churches as His body, unless they are revitalized churches. My vocation takes me to many kinds of churches. In my own times of prayer I often live over again with joy memories of revitalized congregations: a tiny, freshly-whitewashed church in Andhra Pradesh with symbolic patterns of rice grains at its door, its joyful praise accompanied only by a drum and a "squeeze-bos," but overflowing in its personal care for the desperately poor in a *harijan* village; the glad worship of the large, multiracial congregations of Johannesburg and Cape

Town cathedrals, sustaining a bold, costly protest against the harsh injustices of *apartheid*.

On the other hand, I have found churches that are utterly dull and dreary, formal places with no sparkle of glory, no warmth of love overflowing into service. To desert an unloving church is no use, for that will hardly make it any warmer. What do the first have and the second lack? It is, I think, that the first have assimilated and the others have not, the great truth of our union with Christ, conveyed by the images of the Vine and the branches, of the Bride of Christ and the Body of Christ.

How can we live genuinely in union with Christ as members of his body? I have touched on this question more than once already, and I will try to spell it out in the last three chapters. Its practical importance is, I hope, becoming increasingly clear. For, as St. Teresa of Avila, a realist and a woman of prayer, said:

Christ has no body now on earth but yours,
no hands but yours,
no feet but yours,
Yours are the eyes through which Christ looks out
with compassion on the world.
Yours are the feet with which he is to go about doing good.
Yours are the hands with which he is to bless men now.

Living in Christ is, for a Christian, the precondition of caring truly for the world.

"Caring is the greatest thing, caring matters most." These were the words, as he lay dying, of Baron Friedrich von Hügel, a Roman Catholic scholar, who had gone through great difficulties with his Church. From his letters, we can watch him growing in love and wisdom. His last words were spoken to his niece, whom he had guided from an uneasy agnosticism to a life of faith and prayer.

In our exploration into how to help others to become more deeply human, we saw in the last chapter that our caring for them needs to be seen in the context of the Church, the Body of Christ. We now turn to look at our caring in a perspective that extends from the present moment into eternity.

Life beyond death

Many of us do not think much about death, despite the fatal accidents and the violence all around us, or at least we regard it only as a distant hazard.

The possible nearness of death came home to me in a roundabout and rather amusing way. I had been invited to preach the Three Hours' Service on a Good Friday in a country town near where I lived. The rector came and drove me to the church. In the course of my address, I spoke about our Lord's death and of our own deaths. To make my point a little clearer, I said I had enjoyed the drive that morning but of course no one could tell for certain whether I should arrive home alive. As I said that, a smile went round the faces of the entire congregation. I didn't discover what a brick I had dropped until after the service, when in the vestry the rector told me that he had recently had his license endorsed* for dangerous driving.

It is an inescapable fact that each of us is going to die, as are those who are close to us. What is going to happen then to us and to them? I must say frankly, I am sure of very little, but of that little I am convinced. We may speculate. We may perhaps learn something from other faiths or from psychical research, but the only thing I can feel sure about is what is said by Jesus Christ when he spoke, for instance, to the thief who was dying beside him on his cross, "Today you shall be with me in Paradise." In chapter three, I gave reasons for what I have come to believe about Jesus: the divine coming to us through the human. I am convinced that Jesus knows about man and knows about God, and can disclose to us what are the possible relationships between God and man both in this world and in the life to come.

Heaven

Jesus spoke frequently of heaven. Obviously no maps of heaven can be provided, still less an illustrated guide. None of the words we use about heaven, or even those used by our Lord or the New Testament writers, can be literal words, descriptive words; they are symbolic and illuminative. That is inevitable, because all our words have been coined to describe experience human beings have had, terrestrial experience.

If the New Testament speaks about streets of gold, it means that our experience is going to be rich and glorious beyond all we can think or imagine. We haven't adequate

*A notation on the driver's record of a violation.

language to describe it, but we must make the best use we can of our inadequate language. If a Jumbo jet was the first plane ever to fly over a remote Pacific island in Polynesia, and a Polynesian saw it and tried to describe it to his wife, what could he say? He hasn't the right vocabulary, he has no word for "Jumbo," or "jet," or "plane," or anything like it. He has to use his own Polynesian words and say, "Something went over like an immense bird without flapping its wings, but with the sound of a million bees." That is far from an exact description of the plane, but the plane was real. The fact that we can't describe in precise words the heaven Jesus speaks about doesn't mean that the life to come is for us something vague, or uncertain.

What then do we really mean by "heaven"? We do not mean a place, but a relationship. Heaven, I would say, is rejoicing in the friendship of God and in all true love that we have known. True love is always ultimately from God, and as the first letter of John says, "He who lives in love lives in God." Heaven, then, is that kind of relationship which God has already built up with us, prolonged and enriched; it includes within it also our deepest relationships with one another. There will be something dynamic about it, as our love continues to grow in depth and sincerity. Edward King, that wise, lovable Bishop of Lincoln, used to say, "This world is the place to make friendships; the world to come is where we enjoy friendships." At least, we enjoy them in a richer way.

I'm sure also that a view of what heaven is like should never distract us from our responsibilities in this world. On the contrary, it should make us more concerned about justice and righteousness and about caring for people here and now, because this world is given to us as the place to build a society where men and women can love and serve one another, become truly human and grow in confidence and love for God. Believing in the life to come should add impetus to our struggle for what is good.

81

Is heaven for all?

We must not bypass this rather difficult question. Can we be sure that everyone is going to rejoice in the life to come, the consummation of friendship and love? The New Testament seems to me to be not quite clear one way or the other. Some passages speak of all being finally brought into a unity in Christ, and of God being all, in all, through all the Christ has done for us. Other passages, including some words of our Lord in the gospels, warn us that all may not receive this final joy. I find this rather perplexing. But Jesus certainly speaks of the serious consequences of our choices in this life. Perhaps all I can honestly say is this: We should agree that what matters most in life is friendship and love and for this we have to have freedom. There is no love unless you are free to give it and free to withhold it. God in His love gives us our freedom, respects our freedom and so will not, I think, forcibly prevent us from misusing it, even if this means our excluding ourselves from His love.

I must elaborate a little. I cannot find in the New Testament any clear statement that the life to come is a kind of second chance, though our growth in sincerity of love may well be in that life both a purification and an enrichment. This life, it appears, is our chance, and that is why *this* life is so important, why justice here and now, and love and concern, are so important. God will estimate us according to our opportunities. Some of those who have had smaller opportunities may be very far ahead of us. Someone who has had to live with grave psychological handicaps may be much further on than I am, so may a Moslem, if he is true to the light he has received. The same may apply even to an atheist, if he is open and truly seeking for reality. It is, of course, through Christ that all such people are being brought to final joy, because, although they may not recognize him, it is Christ who seeks to enlighten and guide every man. Jesus tells us that some dishonest taxcollectors and prostitutes will be received into the kingdom of heaven before many religious people. Perhaps, some people, considering the economic pressures and other handicaps against them, have tried more than we have and are, in the end, more ready to face up to the truth about themselves. In any event, we should be wise to follow the advice of Paul, "Pass no premature judgment, for the Lord will bring to light what darkness hides, and disclose men's inward motives."

Judgment

While judgment should not frighten us, it is unwise to go about with resentments in our hearts or serious matters on our conscience, because we can never know how unexpectedly the crucial moment of death may come. Judgment is much nearer than we think; in fact, it has begun. We do not have to wait for death or for some judgment after death, because we are judging ourselves now. Each night when we go to sleep we are different from what we were when we woke up that morning, either more open or less open, more loving or less loving. We are sorting ourselves out *now*. What comes in the future will only disclose what we have already become. The New Testament makes that quite clear.

What is even more important is not that we are sorting ourselves out, but that we are influencing the people we meet, even if we meet them only for a short time. We are part of their environment. Each person we meet, we move, even if only a millimeter. We either encourage them to come nearer to fullness of life, or else we repel them from it. That is why, and here I know how seriously I fail, if we are hard and unimaginative, lacking in real listening and understanding, we are pushing people away, instead of drawing them nearer, to reality, to love, and to God.

We ought to be like windows, flung wide open, with the sunshine pouring in to other people, like a Francis of Assisi or a Gladys Aylward or members of the Focolare Movement. But in fact we easily become closed, shut in on ourselves. The windows are not only closed, they are often coated over either by great splashes of mud, our blindness to some injustice around us, or by some longstanding insensitivity within us, or else by the equivalent of an all-pervasive industrial smut, a daily accumulation of little inhumanities, a lack of love-in-action. We know ourselves sufficiently to realize we cannot clean ourselves up. We cannot really open ourselves. Only Love can unloose locked-up love. God's love came and comes to us, in Jesus, to do just that for us. Are we ready to be loved? Facing that question, is a bit demanding.

Present implications

Let us focus our attention on the here and now, and in rather a practical way. Whether we realize it or not, there is a secret struggle going on in your heart and mine, and in the hearts of all men. It is a hidden struggle between love and generosity on the one side and our pride and self-sufficiency on the other; a struggle between some form of our egoism and the influence of the Spirit of Jesus Christ. We are in the middle of that struggle and so are our friends. It is our struggle, but we also wish to help them in theirs.

If we're going to be of use to our friends or ourselves, we must first learn to stand as firmly as we can on whatever convictions we've managed to come to already. Unless we have found a fairly firm footing, we can't give anyone much lasting help, and we shall be of more use if we stand, not grim and long-faced, but in a genial yet resolute way.

Next, what's going to give us strength to stand? Love, I believe, is again the answer. In many situations, it's been somebody's friendship or the love of husband or wife, which has given us strength to stand and to cope. The love of Jesus Christ can be like that, which is why we need to be exposed day by day to his humanizing love through receptive praying.

We need to learn about our Christian faith and the reasons there are for it, but not just in order to "talk religion" (what a bore that can be!), nor to win arguments (often also rather a bore), but to be ready, whenever a question crops up, to have something sensible and reasonable to say.

We must watch that we do not become hard and critical people. If, in our daily jobs we have to evaluate work and other people's capacities, this critical outlook can become "second nature" to us. We easily fall into the habit of speaking critically of people when it's not really necessary. If we do, it is goodbye to being able to help others in the hidden struggles that are going on within them and us.

Above all, let us keep constantly in mind that we can't, in our own strength, give them the kind of help and encouragement they need; of that I am certain. Day by day the love, joy and strength of the Risen Jesus must come flooding into us quietly, like the tide coming in. That is what happens, or what can happen, in prayer. Our help to others depends so much on our relation with God in prayer. He may then be able to use us far beyond what we think.

Lord, make me a bringer of your peace;
Where there is unkindness, let me bring love;
Where there is perplexity, let me bring confidence;
Where there is unhappiness, let me bring joy—
Now and for eternity.

What others choose to do is of course their own responsibility, but our quiet influence, our sincerity, our understanding, our love may be going to make an enormous difference to some people, a difference perhaps not confined to life in this world.

Worship like love is wasting time.

A lover who kept his eye on his watch when he was with his girl, or who calculated what practical good that love would do, would be no lover. Nevertheless, love has its consequences.

Worship is being glad to be with God, forgetting all about the time, and not asking what practical good it will do, though worship also may have momentous consequences. Charles de Foucauld, a "permissive" French foreign legion officer, turned Trappist, turned Sahara hermit, shows us that. At Tamanrasset he built his hermitage, a simple adobe house. At one end he had his altar, where he prayed for four or five hours a day. Beside the door was his chair, and here he sat and received anyone who called, poor Tuaregs or French soldiers or officials, so that he became known as the "universal brother." His being available to God, "*Abba*, Father," for hours at a stretch in prayer made him available to his human brothers who called on him and interrupted him whenever they wished.

All through this book we are concerned with being human and helping others to become truly human. This, too, was our Lord's aim in His life, "I have come that men may have life, and may have it in all its fullness." We do that most effectively, as we have seen in the last two chapters, when we are working together, in a perspective stretching from the present into eternity. We have noticed several times the importance of the life of prayer. In the last three chapters, I should like to gather together my reflections on the intertwined themes of worship, meditation, contemplation, and prayer. The true man of worship is the man of love.

Many people, even sincere Christians, do not see worship like that. When I was teaching in a seminary in New York, I had a student, a good New Testament scholar, a keen Christian, a devoted worker in a Harlem ghetto, who said to me, "I don't see the point of worship of any kind." He never came to our college chapel, nor to any other worship if he could avoid it.

There are now plenty of people like him. They are perhaps not reacting so much against real worship as against its common caricatures, for worship can become an "escapism," like a love affair where the two are entirely absorbed in one another, *égoisme à deux*. It is disastrous when worship is in this way divorced from our present social responsibilities. Worship can also be turned into mere aestheticism. Beauty has an important place in worship, but if beauty becomes an end in itself, the so-called worship becomes aestheticism and nothing more. Sometimes, worship becomes an ecclesiastical "drill," like an oriental court etiquette to a celestial emperor, and that happens particularly when the overwhelming majesty of God is so emphasized as almost to deny his presence within us.

How then can we describe true worship? Like so many other deep experiences, we shall never be able to put it adequately into words. For me, worship is a sense of the wonder of God and of His love, a sense that should then color and transform the rest of the experience of life. (You might think about that and perhaps see if you could put it better.) The essence of worship is, I think, caught by Charles Wesley in his line, "Lost in wonder, love, and praise."

In our corporate services, reflection on the scriptures, intercession and other elements of prayer will normally cluster around worship, but, in my opinion, the sense of worship should be fundamental and infuse color into all the rest. Doubtless it will break through into particular words of worship such as the *Magnificat*, the song of Mary:

My soul doth magnify the Lord,
And my spirit hath rejoiced in God my Savior.

or the *Sanctus*, which is a high point of most forms of the Eucharist:

Holy, holy, holy, Lord God of Hosts;
Heaven and earth are full of thy glory.
Glory be to thee, O Lord most High.

Bishop Kenneth Kirk in his profound book on prayer, *The Vision of God*, said that worship should also be "the culminating moment" of our daily personal prayers. I agree with him.

Why worship?

I have become convinced that if we are going to reach maturity and fullness of life, worship needs to be a part of our daily lives. I see it as an elemental need. Our bodies want food, fresh air, and exercise. Our minds need books to make us think. Our emotional development requires the give-and-take of real companionship. Latent artistic gifts, much more widespread than we think, need surroundings with plenty of artistic stimuli. In just the same way our spiritual capacities need to be drawn out and developed by the right *milieu*, which includes the experience of worship.

That is the meaning of the words in the Fourth Gospel, "God is spirit, and those who worship him must worship in spirit and in truth." That is, we must worship Him in authenticity. God seeks such people to worship Him. We must not misunderstand and think that God wishes people to worship by singing Him songs of flattery. Because God loves people, He wishes them to worship. He knows that worship is for their real good, an element in their becoming truly human. "The living man is the glory of God."

It seems to me one of the saddest aspects of our civilization that many people have not discovered the joy of worship. It is like never having known the joy of friendship and love. It's just hard luck on them. They may only have met the caricatures of worship. Perhaps, as we saw earlier, their capacity for worship has not developed. It sometimes happens, and this needs to be looked at sympathetically, that some have experienced real worship, but now find it has gone dead for them. Many have not discovered a form of worship which meets their needs and their temperaments, though there may be many more options in forms of worship than they imagine.

I should need another book and a larger one to explore all the options, but I must content myself with one group of them, the Eucharist, the Lord's Supper, Holy Communion, or the Mass. It has a bewilderingly rich variety of forms. I should like to say something which is basic to all its forms. In the past, most Roman Catholics and Eastern Orthodox, as well as many Anglicans, have thought of the Eucharist as central to the Christian life. Most other Christians have not, but in worship, as in some other matters, we have come closer to each other in recent years, and are now more ready to explore one another's ways. We all might, therefore, take a fresh look at the eucharist.

The centrality of the Eucharist

Jesus, it seems to me, made the Eucharist central when He said: "Do this in remembrance of me." He said it as He faced His death, His last effort in service of love to men. The fundamental reason why we share in the Eucharist is love, our love responding to Christ's love and His command. Again and again in the New Testament we see the Christians coming together to "do this" in remembrance of Him.

The *Didache*, a Christian document written probably early

in the second century, says, "On the Lord's day come together, break bread and make the eucharist." Justin Martyr in the middle of the same century wrote, "Those who live in cities or in the country" meet together for the Eucharist on the first day of the week, and do so because "Jesus Christ our Savior rose from the dead on that same day." It was a weekly joyful eucharistic feast. Every Sunday an Easter! So it has gone on all down the centuries in the majority of Christian congregations throughout the world. The great reformers, Luther and Calvin, wanted it to go on weekly, but the reaction against medieval abuses made it impossible for them to carry their point. In recent years, however, this weekly Eucharist has increasingly established itself. Roy Strong, the director of the National Portrait Gallery in London, when broadcasting about his job, spoke about how he valued the Sunday Eucharist:

> The week begins for my wife and me with the prayer each Sunday morning which comes at the end of the new communion service which asks God "to send us out into the world to live and work to thy praise and glory." Each week this petition is renewed, leaving one grateful for what he has been got through, sorrowful for what has been neglected, not done or, worst of all, done badly, hopeful that it may be put right. In the hurly-burly of modern life Sunday is recharging day. One never ceases to be amazed how much one is mentally sorted out for the coming week by taking part, along with a congregation of other working people, in the time-hallowed formulae of the liturgy. One draws deep strength and sustaining nourishment from it and one misses it terribly if one cannot, for some reason or another beyond one's control, get there.

The shape of the Eucharist

One reason why many Christians do not see the Eucharist like that is that it has so often become unduly formalized and spoiled with all sorts of needless paraphernalia. Useful simplifications are now coming. Twenty years ago, when the movement for reform was only just starting, I was staying in the Belgian monastery of Mount César at Louvain, and I asked a monk there, one of the greatest scholars in this field, "Father, could you tell me how to explain to ordinary Christians why changes are needed in the Eucharist, and what kind of changes?" I shall never forget the clarity of his reply.

"In early times," he said, "the Eucharist had been like a splendid *salon*, a fine room, well proportioned. Then, as the centuries went by, more furniture was brought in, more pictures, many in good taste individually, but more and more, until you could hardly move about in the *salon*. It was cluttered up. Its clear lines and fine proportions no longer struck you."

I pressed him further, "What then, Father, do you think are the essential principles to retain?"

"There are three," he answered. "First, we must never lose, in our worship, a sense of the reality and wonder of God. Then, we must make it clear that the Eucharist is an action of the whole people in their respective parts, and not just something the priest does. Finally, the Eucharist must have a clear structure, so that everyone can grasp, without too much explanation, what it is all about."

The sense of the reality and wonder of God is a *sine qua non*, something quite indispensable, in all authentic worship—the reality of God over all and in all. This does not depend entirely on how or where the Eucharist is celebrated, whether in a student's study-bedroom or at Chartres Cathedral. It does not depend only, probably not chiefly, on the words. It depends much more on the mentality, the sincerity, indeed on the *love* in the hearts of those who are there. Something may be missing in the printed text; much more may be missing in our hearts.

We must make it clear that the priest or minister does not celebrate the Eucharist for spectators who only watch and listen. The New Testament says that the whole Church is a royal priesthood, so we all join in our respective parts in celebrating the Eucharist. One of the good features of the revised forms of the Eucharist in many parts of Christendom is that they make that clear.

Next, the Eucharist should have an obvious shape or structure, so that you can see what you are about. The monk went on to explain that every Eucharist was a double feasting, a feasting on the scriptures as the Word of God and then a feasting on the sacrament.

We have to see that the first part of the service is not jammed up with subsidiary elements. What has to be clear is that it is a feasting on the scriptures. It is not a Bible class, where you go primarily to learn more facts. It is a feast, as you speak of a feast of music. You let the scriptures do something to you. It's the same as going to a concert, or a festival; something happens to you. As you come away, you realize that, at least in some small degree, you are more human, you are more open to life.

The address at the Eucharist, as well as the readings, should help to make it a feast. When I was staying at a small Roman Catholic abbey in New York State, the abbot at mass invited us, as we sat around the altar, to say how the gospel we had just heard spoke to us in the circumstances of our daily lives. He was a wise and tactful man. If anyone had rather too much to say, the abbot would quietly interrupt and say, "Thank you, we will bear that in mind." At the end he summed up our reflections in barely two dozen words. It really was a feasting together.

The second part of the eucharist is essentially four actions. We could say that the Eucharist is something *done* rather than something *said*. After all, our Lord säid *"Do* this." It might be better if we were less verbose; we chatter too much to God. We want more silence, silence for reflection, silence for the love which is too deep for words. The four actions are what Jesus himself did when he gave us the Eucharist: He took bread and wine, He blessed God, He broke the bread, He gave to the disciples the bread and wine.

First, we put the bread and wine on the altar-table. Worship is love, and that is why it should gather up into itself all the details of daily life as love always wishes to do. Bread, the symbol of the labor of our daily life, and the sparkling wine of life's joy and freshness we want to put into God's hands as expressions of our love to Him, and for Him to use to bring love to others: "Offer your very selves to Him."

Secondly, we bless God. We thank him for all he has done, is doing and will do for us through Christ. Jesus did that at the last supper, just as at solemn Jewish meals the father of the family gave thanks for all God had done for His people. The word "eucharist" of course means "thanksgiving," just that. Thanking God is the central prayer of the Eucharist. It has taken on a thousand forms down through the centuries. It has been called in our various traditions the great thanksgiving, the *anaphora*, the canon of the Mass, and the prayer of consecration.

Thirdly, the one bread is broken ready to be shared by those present. By that we are reminded of the depth of our fellowship one with another. If here we are united to the Lord, we are united to one another in Him. "When we break the bread, is it not a means of sharing in the body of Christ? Because there is one loaf, we, many as we are, are one body, for it is one loaf of which we all partake."

Fourthly, the bread and wine are given to those who are there. All that is essential in the Eucharist are the four actions, which speak for themselves. As we do them, we open ourselves by faith to be united to our Lord and to one another in Him. For He, who is with us at all times and in all places, is present with us in a special way in the Eucharist, or possibly we should say He is, in a special way, active among us. Once more all human words—"present," "active"—are inadequate to convey the reality we wish to speak about. We can't avoid words, we must carefully choose the most adequate words, and yet remember their limitations. The words which we usually translate "Do this in remembrance of me," probably do not mean simply "Remember Christ and do this in memory of Him," but rather, "When you do this, then the events of the past, Christ's living, dying, and rising again are with all their power brought to you in the present moment." There is also in the Eucharist a real anticipation of the final gathering together of all things into Christ. As C. H. Dodd has written, "Past, present and future are indissolubly united in the sacrament."

It is difficult to describe exactly what is meant, but there are analogies in human friendship and love. Sometimes memories of shared experiences come back to us, not as mere memories, but with some of the reality and power of the original events. Sometimes eagerly awaited events give us in anticipation some of their real joy and strength already.

The bread and wine have a very important place within the whole action, and that is why they are spoken of as "the body and blood of Christ." That cannot, of course, be meant literally; though when we speak of a spiritual presence, we do not mean something vague or in any way doubtful. It is something at once as real and intangible as friendship and love. As a handshake is to friendship, and an embrace is to love, so is the bread and wine to the spiritual reality of Christ. Each of the outward signs is distinct from, yet expresses and also conveys, the intangible, and the intangible in each instance is deeply real.

We are perhaps, worried at times because we have no feeling of the presence of Christ at Holy Communion. The reason may be that we have allowed some disloyalty to Him to become a barrier between Him and us. But often this lack of feeling comes from no fault of ours. A true man of prayer, who had made many sacrifices for the love of God, once said paradoxically that the reality of Christ is something too deep to be felt. That statement may need some qualification. While it is largely true, yet at times contact with Christ at a deep level within us actually wells up into our feelings. However, we cannot test the depth of our communion with the Lord, either at the Eucharist or anywhere else, by the vividness of our feelings. We know the reality, not through our feelings, but through the Lord's promise to be with us.

In recent years, more frequent Holy Communion has come to be valued by many people. This is good. The only danger I see is that we could take it "for granted," as we so easily take for granted our friends and families. It is essential that we find some way of getting ourselves ready for the Holy Communion so that it remains as real and significant to us as our Lord's coming was to the disciples on the first Easter day.

Forms of the Eucharist

"Do this in remembrance of me." Was ever another command so obeyed? Many Christians have found in the Holy Communion their strength and joy. Sunday by Sunday it has sustained them. They have gone to Holy Communion on days when an important decision had to be made. On the day of their marriage they have received Holy Communion together. The sacrament has been brought to them when they were ill. It will be brought to them when they are about to pass through death. It is woven into life.

The Eucharist is not dull routine. It is an action of love. It is the giving of ourselves to the Lord for Him to take hold of us, to enrich us with His love, to remake us, and humanize us. The Eucharist takes on as many forms as making friends and growing in love do. It is never quite the same. It becomes deeper and is something surprisingly different. So we need to keep awake to many facets of the splendor of the Eucharist.

Shall I never forget the wonder of the Orthodox liturgy in great gilded churches in Moscow, the singing of the choir with deep basses like the swell of the sea, the massive congregations standing shoulder to shoulder, a togetherness which could be felt. Those were people of courage, facing, if not persecution, unjust discrimination because of their faith, yet there they were, supported by the love of the Lord, the Bridegroom of His faithful on earth and in heaven. Indelible, too, in my memory is a Mass in a tiny, sweltering church on a small Caribbean island. There were men, women and children, all very poor, packed together, singing with a rhythm quite irresistible, then prostrate in a deep tangible silence. It was like the apostolic church, "not many wise," for it was "to shame the wise that God has chosen what the world counts folly." I remember also in a Malawi village saying the Mass on the sawn-off stump of a tree as an altar in the cool, early light of dawn. Then, in a garden at Santa Barbara against the fantastic colors of a California sunset, I celebrated a Eucharist which we had worked hard all day to compose. A Eucharist in a cave in the Orange Free State brought back memories of the tough pioneers, the first missionary community in those parts, for whom the cave was both home and chapel. They were memories of faith amid hardship. Then, that was a homely yet real Eucharist on an ordinary kitchen table, the morning sunshine pouring in and the day's work about to start. "He was known to them in the breaking of the bread." Indeed, was ever another command so lovingly obeyed?

Christ with us in life

These times of Eucharistic communion, in all their variety, are precious to us, but in fact worship, the Eucharist, is as wide as life. "Whoever eats my flesh and drinks my blood dwells continually in me and I dwell in him." As we go from the altar-table to our dinner tables with our families and friends, He goes with us to bring through us His joy, His love, His strength, ". . . that my joy may be in you and your joy complete." As we go to our hundreds of kinds of leisure, which Josef Pieper has called "the basis of culture," the Risen Christ is with us, as He walked to Emmaus with two friends on Easter day. He goes with us to our work as well, and we know He is there as really as He was when He stood at a carpenter's bench or in a crowd of sick people. As we struggle against the forces of evil, we need never feel alone; He is with us still. He died to break the grip of evil and rose again to unleash new energies of love. We offer Him our very selves. He draws us into himself and gives us a new potential of humanness and love. That is "worship offered by mind and heart."

Worship is the energizing focus of the totality of our lives and service. It can never be narrow and confined, whether in a back room, a downtown church or an African hut. Worship is something enormous. It is as wide as our lives, as wide as the world.

It would be no good my pretending to be a cool detached observer when it comes to the Bible. I simply love the Bible. I could not get along without it. Even when God meant almost nothing to me, Jesus meant a great deal, and I fell for Paul when I was twelve! For years I earned my bread and butter by lecturing on the New Testament; it was for me not a job but a delight.

I am well aware, of course, that many people, including some Christians, do not share my love of the Bible. I can understand why. The miracles discredit it for some of them, and it comes from an age very different from our own in mental and social presuppositions. Though they might not put it so crudely, they are like the boy who bought a Bible at a secondhand bookshop and then turned up again five minutes later and said: "Could I please change this Bible for another book more up to date?" That the Bible does speak to many modern and intelligent men and women, however, is indisputable.

Of course Christians have made, and sometimes still do make, wild claims for the Bible. We must not exaggerate. The Bible is human as well as divine. It is in some ways like our Lord Himself. In fact, the Bible is for some people not only human, but too crudely human. There is no Victorian refinement there. Look at the cynicism of Ecclesiastes, at the passionate love poetry of the Song of Songs, at unedifying stories in Old Testament history, and a touch of human vengefulness even in the New Testament in some of the latter parts of the Apocalypse. In spite of those strange passages, however, God with His love breaks through in the Bible to give us light, warmth, and humanness.

Whatever some of the original authors may have had in mind, the Jewish religious leaders and later the Christian churches gradually selected those particular books to form the Bible, to show us God and His care for us. The selection as we now have it was completed by A.D. 400.

There has been a great amount of fine spiritual writing since then, and we ought to make better use of it, but these books of the Bible are for us basic. Some tell us why they were written originally. The author of the Fourth Gospel, for example, says that he wrote to help us to put our confidence in Jesus the Christ, the Son of God, and so in this way to receive life, that fullness of life Jesus came to bring. Those words might well stand as the underlying aim of the whole Bible: that we should come to our full humanity through trusting ourselves confidently to God, the God who has disclosed Himself supremely in Jesus Christ.

There is, then, in the Bible the human and the divine and no sharp line can be drawn between them. The Bible can rightly be used in different ways. I should like, though, to make a rough distinction between Bible-study and Bible-praying. In the first, we look more at its human side: Who were the authors? What human situations faced them? In the second, we try mainly to pierce through the human to the divine. I will also say a few words on the Bible in corporate worship.

Bible study

It is almost impossible to write in a few pages anything worth reading about Bible study, yet I must try, because unless we know something about the human setting of these books, we may get things seriously distorted when we look for the divine.

100

We need God's disclosure of Himself in Jesus, but to receive it at all adequately we have to know what the Bible is. How far, for example, are the gospels accurate historical accounts of what Jesus said and did? Are they commentaries on his life or meditations about his life?

Jesus does not stand by Himself. His own life of prayer had many of its roots in the Old Testament. He is the culmination, so we Christians believe, of a development which runs through the whole of the Old Testament. Still less can we understand Jesus if we do not see Him in the life, reflections, and meditations of His followers all through the New Testament.

Let us in passing notice one practical matter. We may find the Bible cropping up in conversation. Some people may talk as if there were hardly any human element in it at all; others may try to dismiss it as a collection of legends and useless speculations. Without pretending to be experts, we ought, again, to be sufficiently trained to have something sensible to say.

First, the Bible is not a book but a library, and a varied one. Its books cannot be forced into a straitjacket. Some obviously are history books. The account of the intrigues of David's court, for example, is reliable history. Not all that looks like history, however, *is* history. There is poetry, such as much of what the prophets wrote. It is important to read this *as* poetry, because the truth of life is too rich and wonderful to be conveyed entirely in the prose of history. We need imagery, we need poetry. There are legal books and plenty of letters. It is a fascinating library. Clearly, many passages of the Bible are parables, not only in the gospels, but also in the Old Testament. The creation stories in Genesis are parables with fundamental principles in them. The intriguing story of Jonah is a parable with a permanent message as clear as the parable of the Good Samaritan. The lover of the Bible is set free from many difficulties by this approach to the scriptures.

Secondly, the span of time between the earliest and the

101

latest books is about the same as that between the Norman conquest of England and ourselves, and in that length of time a great deal can happen. That fact was once rather amusingly illustrated in a school. In religious education one day a class read a primitive, vengeful story from the book of Judges, with God appearing to encourage the slaughter. The next week, when they read the passage from the first letter of John saying that God is love, one girl spoke her thoughts aloud, "But hasn't God improved since last time!" It is not that God improves, but that men's eyes are gradually opened. That is why we are not worried by primitive stories in the Bible.

Thirdly, we turn again to the most crucial Biblical problem. Have we a sufficiently accurate record of Jesus' teaching in the gospels? That really amounts to three questions: Have errors slipped into the manuscripts while they were being copied out by hand and when they were being translated? Have recent discoveries in Palestine shown the gospels to be inaccurate? May not distortions have come in when the sayings were still being passed on by word of mouth before they were committed to writing at all? I will deal here only with the first three gospels, because the Fourth Gospel is probably nearer to an inspired meditation than to an account of Jesus' life.

We don't have the original manuscripts, our oldest complete manuscripts must have been copied and recopied dozens of times, and many of them are translations from the original Greek. Mistakes must inevitably have crept in. But, we have many more manuscripts of the New Testament than of other comparably ancient books and ours are much nearer in date to the original writing. The major manuscripts date from the fourth century, that is, three hundred years after the writing of the New Testament books, although scraps of the New Testament on papyri, which have been discovered in the dry sands of Egypt, probably date to the first half of the second century. Therefore, although slips have crept in, we have so many good documents that we can check one against another and eliminate the errors. We can say with some confidence that we can reconstruct the text of the gospels almost as the original authors wrote them.

Another question is raised: have recent discoveries in Palestine, particularly the Dead Sea Scrolls, shown that the gospels give an accurate picture of Jesus? An attempt was made to interpret the scrolls in that way, but it was countered effectively by a letter in the London *Times* signed by ten New Testament scholars of international reputation, both Jewish and Christian. The Dead Sea Scrolls are really about a Jewish ascetic group, the Essenes, which existed a little earlier than New Testament times. Since we had known something about them for a long time through the Jewish historian, Josephus, the scrolls tell us about the background of those times, but they do not give us a new picture of Jesus, nor undermine the reliability of our record of his words.

A further question must be faced: did the account of our Lord's teaching become seriously distorted during the thirty or so years while it was being passed on by word of mouth between our Lord's own speaking and the writing of the first copies of the gospels? When we compare minutely the records in the first three gospels, it looks as if the teaching was modified as its implications were applied to different situations. We should expect that. However, the first Christians were a truth-loving people and would at least try to preserve a reliable picture of our Lord and his teaching. Scholars have examined the matter with great care. One of the most meticulous New Testament scholars, Joachim Jeremias, has shown that the first three gospels have preserved the teaching of Jesus both in style and content as something quite distinctive from the rest of the New Testament writings. At many points we can check that Jesus' teaching has *not* been greatly accommodated to the needs or moods of the early Church. So Professor Jeremias, turning the tables on the extreme critics, concludes that in the first three gospels, "it is the inauthenticity, and not the authenticity, of the sayings of Jesus that must be demonstrated."

So much for the general reliability of our records of the teaching of Jesus.

For our New Testament study in general, we must remember that the books are not meant to provide us with exact solutions to our contemporary problems. Their purpose is to communicate to us the vitality, the *élan*, of the first Christian communities, not to answer our problems. Krister Stendahl, Dean of the Harvard Divinity School, has warned us against "a too close-sighted view" of scripture. He has reminded us that "the distance between the first and the twentieth century has drastically widened," and so all our thinking and praying "has to come to terms with this distance." Let us be precise: There are some areas of social life where we can no longer accept literally the New Testament teaching. Slaves, for example, are advised to accept their present position. Passive submission to practically all authority is taken for granted. Women are to accept their customary rôle in first-century society and not to expect more. What is said about relations between husbands and wives, children and parents, inevitably lacks those insights into human nature which we have gained over the last fifty years. In other words, the New Testament everywhere assumes the mental furniture of the first century. Further, the Christians were, at that time, so tiny a minority that, whatever they might have thought, they couldn't have influenced the social structures of their day. In the New Testament there are, however, time bombs, social explosives, as, for example, Paul's statement, "There is no such thing as Jew and Greek, slave and freeman, male and female; for you are all one person in Christ Jesus."

People should, as far as they can, study the historical issues in the scriptures, even if their chief concern may be to use the Bible in their life of prayer. Real prayer must have firm, historical foundations and not be floating about in some cloud-cuckoo land. Some people find Bible study groups stimulating, especially to give them an initial impulse, but such groups should not, I think, replace our individual use of the Bible. That is part of our keeping ourselves "open to

God," as we take trouble to keep in touch with close friends. I should like to suggest at least half an hour's serious study each weekend. There are many books to help us. A small book that can open up the study of the Bible in our contemporary setting is William Neil's *The Truth about the Bible*. Many people find the epistles difficult, but they are essential if we are going to understand our Lord and His impact on the early Christian communities. The best introduction to them is still, I think, J. B. Phillips' *Letters to Young Churches*, which pioneered the present wave of new translations. The Bible as a whole is fairly massive and to many a confusing maze. Bishop Stephen Neill in his *One Increasing Purpose*, a course of daily readings for three months, gives us a golden thread through the Old and New Testaments, which may make us lifelong Bible lovers.

The Bible in corporate worship

When Christians hear the Bible read in worship, they are hearing about themselves and their family history. The Bible is a library about God and His agelong purpose for His people. It has been, and always is, a purpose of love. We see God choosing as his people the descendants of Abraham. They were never meant to be an inward-looking élite. He intended to make them into a community who would then share his love with all humanity, "a light to all peoples, a beacon for the nations." The history of the Hebrew people is the story of how God prepared and disciplined his people for their immense task, which would involve openness to the world and suffering. The Hebrew people were free to refuse that responsibility and in general, so it appears to Christians, did refuse it. Then, in the gospels, we see Jesus and His disciples accepting the responsibility, but the disciples deserted, and God's universal purpose narrowed down to just one person, Jesus. Unswervingly loyal to God's purpose of love, He went to the cross on Good Friday. Then at Easter He was alive again and the disciples gathered round Him. Strengthened by His Spirit, they became the new people to share God's light and love with all nations, until God carries out His purpose to gather together all things into one in Christ.

When Bible passages are read to us in worship, we should place them where they fit into the agelong story of God's caring for His people and for the world. This is why preparatory Bible study is so important. The scripture readings in worship are not the kind of reading and explanation we have in a classroom or lecture room, nor are they pictures from the past which we look at from a distance. They are a drama, a drama not to watch, but one to take part in. When we hear the Bible in worship, we are considering our predecessors' disloyalties so we may repent of our own. We are being brought into a special closeness with the Lord and are being remagnetized by his love. We are being drawn out of ourselves and caught up into the living drama of God's love for humanity. We should then go out from the drama into God's world, more realistic and more loving.

This should be true of any biblical service, such as the matins and evensong of the Anglican church, and particularly of the first part of the Eucharist, the feast of the Word. The same thing happens to us, as we have seen, in the second part of the Eucharist, the feast on the sacrament. We are drawn into our Lord's loving, dying, rising, and going forth again into the world. We are there at the last supper, there at the cross, there on Easter morning, there at the coming of the Spirit.

> Send us out into the world
> in the power of thy Spirit.

We shall probably not be sent out effectively into the world through our sharing in the feast of the Word and of the sacrament, however, unless we first learn individually how to be "fed and nourished" by the scriptures. You cannot participate actively in a great symphony unless you practice regularly on your own instrument at home.

Personal Bible-praying

Much turns on personal Bible-praying. I know this from my own experience, and many of my friends say the same thing. There are all sorts of ways of going about it. Trying to help others has at least shown me that. Perhaps the most useful thing I can do is to speak about my own experience, for what it is worth. I had better say at once that I haven't always managed very well. Sometimes, in fact, I have been inclined to give up, but somehow I carried on and now I am very glad that I did. Here, therefore, is my experience, the experience of quite an ordinary person. Think it over for yourself. The only way to find the best method for you is to make your own exploration. I wish you a good journey.

While I have suggested Bible study once a week, I would recommend Bible-praying every day, if possible. We are not, in Bible-praying, primarily trying to learn more facts, but rather to be more with our Lord, to love more deeply. Normally for this, I turn to passages which I know by experience speak to me: usually the gospels, parts of the epistles, verses of the Psalms, and sometimes other bits of the Old Testament. (Perhaps I should say that as an Anglican priest I read most of the Old Testament and all the New Testament regularly in the course of the year at our daily morning and evening services. That forms the background and perspective to all my use of the Bible.) In my Bible-praying I don't think of the passage as a chapter of a history book, or as a newspaper article, but rather like a letter from a close friend. If your friend has discovered how to write, you don't read the letter and throw it at once into the wastepaper basket. You put it in your wallet or in your handbag. You read it over again. You think about your friend. That letter is, in a way, a written meeting. If we love our Lord, many of us are glad to meet Him again and again in those well-loved places. For me, one story from the gospels is enough, or just a few verses. Sometimes it's only one phrase, like a phrase in a friend's letter that keeps coming back to mind.

Everyone must find his own time for Bible-praying. There are obvious advantages in having a regular time, if it is possible. Some people find it useful to drop into a church during the day; no telephone or door bell will ring there. Some find their minds are quieter, steadier for prayer in the evening, but mine is usually too drowsy for this kind of praying then. The best plan for me is to read over the passage before I go to sleep; it seems to "simmer" in my mind during the night. Then I do my Bible-praying the next morning. I suppose husband and wife or two friends could do the preliminary reading together, and that might be quite a good idea.

I remember the priest who started me off with Bible-praying when I was a student. I think of him often with gratitude and affection. He taught me to settle myself down fairly quickly, to imagine the story from the gospel, to reflect on its implications for myself, to pray about it in my own words, or just to be quiet without words, and then, towards the end of my prayer, to decide to do something practical about it, so as to keep the whole thing down to earth. I went on in roughly the same pattern for some years.

Picturing our Lord as being with me, as He was with the disciples in the gospels, was the first part of Bible-prayer that began to fade out. Of course, while I had always known that to picture our Lord did not bring Him any nearer to me; for quite a long time it did help me to focus my attention with love on Him, and it still helps me occasionally in that way. That applies, I think, to any use of our imagination in prayer.

Next, as I became more familiar with Bible passages, I found that thinking out their implications became less real and less helpful. The result was that my Bible-praying became more and more having a sense of the Lord's presence, praying in my own words, and sometimes saying only a few words very slowly, such as "Lord, I trust you, I mean to trust you more, for you mean a great deal to me."

At the stage of my life when this was happening, I read,

108

quite by chance, of another pattern of Bible-praying which was summarized in three phrases:

> Christ before me,
> Christ within me,
> Christ through me.

I decided to try it and it turned out to be very useful to me for another spell of years. I continued to read my few verses—I still do—each night, but it didn't bother me if my next morning's praying was not closely linked with that passage. It normally worked out rather like this: Usually, I would begin by saying, "Yes, Lord, you are before me. You are actually with me." Then I might reflect on the words that I had read the night before; or more often I would simply say something like this, "You said that to your disciples and now you are with me, always with me." Then I would just try to be still. Next, and sometimes quite quickly, I would pass on to the words "Christ within me." We have to use words like "within" or "in," but there is no word adequate to describe how close He is. "Christ is nearer to us than we are to ourselves." Anyway, such New Testament passages seemed to come up within me, "Through faith may Christ dwell in your hearts in love"; "Whoever eats my flesh and drinks my blood dwells continually in me and I dwell in him." Quietly and slowly, I would try to grasp that, as Christ dwells in me, so His strength, His love, Hs joy must be in me. I would try to be relaxed and not to worry about how I could get through all the work I had to do that day. "I have strength for anything through him who gives me power." As Christ's love was within me, I would ask myself, "Need I still worry about being able to cope with so-and-so?" I saw that I must do what I could, I must try not to become tense, but rather to let Christ's love which is in me come through me. If I could go on doing that, Christ's love would gradually change me from inside, "Here and now, dear friends, we are God's children; what we shall be has not yet been disclosed, but we know that when it is disclosed we shall be like Him." I had to realize, too, that His joy was already with me—"that my joy may be in you and your joy complete." Of course, I knew that, like everybody else, I should have depressions, sorrows, partings, frustrations, and all the rest. How well we all know that! Within us, however, there is the spring of His joy, always welling up, always flowing, though sometimes out of sight, under our sorrows—and if we are not sometimes sorrowful, we aren't human. "Sorrowful," said Paul, "yet always rejoicing."

Christ before me, Christ within me, then Christ through me. Yes, through me He would like to go to wherever I have to go today: to my desk to answer those letters, to that group of students I've been asked to speak to, to that routine job that has to be done. The question is not: "What must I try to do for Christ?" but "What does He want to bring into those situations through me?" It may not be words. It certainly is love.

I am very far from succeeding, but I go on trying. To build up a relationship of real human love and trust often takes a long time. Despite my failures, something else seems to have been happening to my Bible-praying during the last few years. Of course, I do not know how long it will go on. Perhaps something else quite unexpected may happen. But whatever passage I now start from the night before, in the morning my prayer nearly always comes back to words like: "God is love; and His love was disclosed to us in this: He sent his only Son into the world to bring us life. The love I speak of is not our love for God, but the love He showed to us," or to a sentence from the letter to the Galatians: "Now that you have come to know God, or rather to be known by God."

Paul's words mean that we have now come to the realization that we are loved personally by God. In that passage "to know" does not mean only to know intellectually, but to love and to possess, as husband and wife should know one another in their life together. What all that adds up to is, I suppose, that without my planning it, my prayer has come round to the kind of simple contemplative praying I wrote about at the end of chapter three. What I must now try to explore is how to realize more deeply that I am loved by God, how to go on exposing myself to His love and responding to Him in love. I must find out how that love can find expression in my caring more effectively for those around me, how I can care truly for the world in its problems, and, indeed, how to live in this love. "Dwell in my love."

I'm not good at it. I don't find it easy. I find, as others do, that in prayer my mind may go off at a tangent to other things and other people. If so, I often pray for them for a few minutes. While this doesn't seem to me to break up or spoil my prayers, there are people who let themselves get annoyed with distractions. St. Francis de Sales once said that, if in our prayer we are distracted a hundred times, this doesn't matter very much, providing we don't get upset with ourselves. After each distraction, he told us, come back quietly to God. Then there's nothing to worry about, he said, because by doing that we're giving God a hundred signs of our love. God sees we are trying to love him "in and above all things."

Noise or other unfavorable conditions are not necessarily an obstacle to prayer. Once, I was staying with the Little Brothers of Jesus, a modern Roman Catholic community inspired by Charles de Foucauld. They were at St. Maximin near Aix-en-Provence. About half-a-dozen of them lived on the middle floor of a shabby apartment house in a crowded quarter and went out to work during the day. When they came home, we all spent an hour of silent prayer in a small room which they had turned into an oratory. You never heard such a noise from the crowds and children in the street! It was too hot to close the windows. Our neighbors in the floor above always seemed to be shifting furniture about or dropping things on the floor. You couldn't think of anywhere less "suitable" for prayer, but I found those times golden hours. Somehow, the noise was a stimulus to prayer.

Here was a world so close and so obviously needing our prayer. How could we become channels of God's love to the world, through intercession or through neighborly caring, unless we found out how to be with Jesus, to abide in Him among all the noise and racket?

I do not know how I am getting on with that kind of praying. I do not believe in being too introspective. It's not much good pulling up a plant to see whether its roots are growing. All I can say is, I know how much I miss the morning prayer time, if for some reason or other I cannot fit it in. I feel as if I have missed a meal, or a letter, or a visit from a friend. I hope it is all gradually making me rather more human, more aware of the needs of others, and of the opportunities and problems of the world of today.

I would give almost anything to help others to explore these varied, criss-cross paths of Bible-praying.

Prayer has a fascination, no doubt about it, and, today, for quite unexpected people, even for some who might call themselves agnostic. I do not know how many times I have been asked, "I'm very uncertain about God, but I want to pray; do you think I could do it honestly?" You may have friends like that. It was that very question that led me to speak about my own experience at the beginning of this book. When I myself was uncertain, I prayed; looking back, I'm sure I was right. All my subsequent experience leads me to say, "Yes, by all means pray, even if you are praying in an unconventional, unusual way."

My advice would always be: pray, in any possible way you can, but never run away from your intellectual problems. Find someone you can talk them over with. Continue to face them. Don't be afraid of them. Keep your intellectual integrity.

If you can't pray now, in the sense of speaking to God in words of prayer, then reflect on life. That is a kind of praying. Look at the coming day in the best light you have. Think in the spirit of Jesus about people you will probably meet. I should call that prayer, even if some people wouldn't. It may merge eventually into the more usual kinds of prayer as the colors of the spectrum merge into one another.

Go out and meet people. Listen to them, try to understand their *real* needs. In that way, I believe that you are actually meeting God, for He is not only "over all but *in* all," even though you may not realize it. Perhaps at moments you may have an intimation that there is more to it than a human person-to-person relationship.

My hope and prayer is that, somehow, you will become aware of God. It is rather like human friendship. First, we may go about with quite a number of people; then we gradually become aware of two or three of them, or especially of one of them. Out of that awareness there emerges friendship, joy, and love, sometimes almost imperceptibly. A similar awareness may dawn on you if you want to pray, I speak out of my own experience, even while you are finding it difficult to believe. I have suggested something definite you can start on, and this all makes more sense when we remind ourselves of what praying really is.

Praying and asking

Prayer is not, primarily, asking anything from God, although if often appears to be. Prayer is entering into friendship with God; *a real relationship* between God and ourselves is steadily being built up, deep and meaningful. That is almost incredible because God, who is the Lord of the universe, who must be infinitely beyond us, in His love desires our friendship. We can only accept that truth, because Jesus has come and disclosed to us—as far as ever this can be done in human experience—what God actually is. God, He said, is like an Eastern mother who searches all over her house for the *one* silver coin which has broken off her necklace; God is like the father who ran down the road to embrace his returning son. We could never have guessed that. It amounts to this: each time we pray sincerely, God is there first to welcome and receive us. If we forget that, the heart goes out of prayer.

114

Unfortunately, so many books, so many instructions, give almost the opposite impression: that in prayer we have to struggle on and on, that it is hard, uphill work, we have to do ourselves. The truth is just the opposite. "We love, because He first loved us."

Of course, prayer, like love, will afterward involve some effort, but we do not mind that, when we can see the effort is an expression of our deep gratitude for the fact that we have already been welcomed and accepted by the divine love.

By prayer we enter more and more deeply into the continuing friendship to which God welcomes us. Or, to put the same idea into other familiar words, by prayer we abide as branches in Christ, the True Vine. There is no fruit, no sparkling wine of love, unless we dwell in Him and He dwells in us. It is for the sake of those we care for, those whom society treats unjustly, that we plan to live continually in the True Vine. Once more, that does not mean running away from life; it means living in the Vine in the middle of the contemporary world. But that, I think, involves some planning in our life of prayer.

Set times or not?

"Are regular times of prayer absolutely essential," I am often asked, "or is it enough to set aside time specifically for prayer when there are special needs, but in normal circumstances to pray as we go about our work?" I have come to the convicton, as I indicated in chapter two, that, normally, regular times are essential.

I agree that we should also try to pray while we are working. We can't of course always do that, when, for instance, we are making a difficult calculation or driving a car in the rush hour. But it is particularly useful to train ourselves, as we go about our work, to express our confidence in God quite frequently, in short phrases like, "The Lord is my strength and my song." Trust in God will then not remain merely an idea in our minds, but will sink down into our whole being and may eventually become almost "second nature" to us. We shall find ourselves turning often to God with spontaneous words during the day. That makes a great deal of difference. It is like husbands and wives or close friends remembering one another during their work; they say, "I was thinking of you so much today." Such thoughts are likely to be fairly superficial, however, unless, as we have said before, they grow out of times of real companionship, alone with each other. Such times deepen love and help to keep it alive all day long. Our regular times of prayer are like those times alone together. If, occasionally, we have to miss a time of prayer, then that will not matter so much, if we are building up a deep relation with God through a regular rhythm of prayer.

Again, let us remember Jesus. Few of us are busier than He was. Sometimes He didn't have time for meals. He was deeply involved in people's problems, yet He made times to be alone with God. He found a quiet spot early in the morning; sometimes He spent a whole night in prayer, and in the middle of His work he looked up to God with words of trust on His lips. Out of His communion with God, day by day, there welled up the strong and unceasing love He had for men and women, a love which helped them discover their true selves and to become more human.

If we are going to help others as Jesus did, we need, underneath all we do, some plan for our life of prayer. It should be flexible, not too demanding, but definitely *there*— what Dietrich Bonhoeffer called the "hidden discipline." Details will have to be different for each of us.

Basically, we need three elements in our plan. My own experience and my talking with others have now convinced me of that. First, we need at least one time of corporate worship a week, if possible, some kind of Eucharist, as we saw in chapter eight. Next, we need a quiet time every day, as I suggested in the last chapter. Finally, we ought to have a second time of prayer each day, probably in the evening, a gathering up of our reflections on the day.

Does that sound unrealistic, too much? It's no good playing at being in love. It's no good playing at prayer.

There is one element more. I will speak of it later.

An evening time of prayer

Once we are really aware of God's love for us disclosed in Jesus, and once we want to respond to Him with our love in life and in prayer, then we shall find it natural to turn to Him at the end of the day. It is like turning to someone we love. We need it, we want it.

If we are having to work late, or if we are going out and coming back late, it is best to try to find ten minutes early in the evening. At weekends and on holidays, when we have more time, we should feel like spending extra time with Him, who is coming to mean more and more to us. Even at times of great pressure, on the other hand, when we go to bed exhausted, we should have a few moments with Him, just to express in words or in silence our love and our confidence in Him. Brief prayer is far better than no prayer.

Each must discover for himself the best way or the best ways for his evening prayers, for the prayers will vary with the demands life makes on his energies: physical, intellectual, and emotional. Neither in friendship, love, nor prayer should we get "set in a routine." Perhaps, if I share with you my normal experiences, they will suggest ideas to you.

I try to settle down quietly. I realize the presence of God. He is my Lord; He is around me like the air I breathe; He is within me. There may be noises going on or other distractions, but they do not and cannot separate me deep down from Him, "Lord, it is good to be here." "In quietness and confidence shall be your strength."

I can't divide up my praying into compartments, any more than if I were talking over the past day with a close friend. If there is something very pressing on my mind, I begin with that. Normally, however, I start by expressing in words or in wordless silence my appreciation, my love, my adoration of Him. Then, I express the gratitude that is in my heart, for things that have turned out well, for kindnesses I have received, for my friends. I also consider what has not gone well, and why; the ways I have failed others, the ways in which I must have disappointed God. "Be gracious to me, O God, in thy true love."

Then I speak to Him about my needs: for help in a piece of work, for sensitivity to understand someone, for courage and so on. I know from what Jesus has said that I'm not telling God anything He doesn't know already, nor does God need any reminding. I do not have to persuade Him with my words, nor could I. Then why ask Him at all for what I need? I ask because I want to love Him, and to love Him means that I have to open myself honestly to Him, my fears, my joys, my needs. Prayer, like love, requires a courageous honesty. I must acknowledge my angry impulses, too. Don Camillo's words of hatred for the Communist mayor, said before the altar, were not blasphemies, but authentic prayer. We love God, we honor God, but we need not bother about being too polite before God. As we speak, he loves. "God does not ask us to tell him our needs that he may learn about them, but that we may be capable of receiving what he is preparing to give," that great lover of God, St. Augustine, tells us.

We speak to God not only about our needs, but about our fellow men and women, and about our friends. How could we not do so? How could our thoughts and our prayers not turn to them, as we now turn to God, who has made us aware of them in a new way? They may be thousands of miles away, but we are close to them and they to us, for we are all in Him whose presence and love penetrates all. He can use our desires and prayers, as much as our actions and our letters, to convey His sustaining love to them.

Our love for our friends overflows into care for others. As we pray for those who are dear to us, our love and prayer spread out to those who have no friends, to families without much love, to those who lack food or a roof over their heads, to the lonely in prisons, to those who live in fear and under injustice. We pray also for those who exercise that power which easily, but not inevitably, corrupts. We desire that they should be human and treat others as fully human. Jesus came that "men may have life and may have it in all its fullness." *Abba*, Father, may that be so.

In my personal praying, I sometimes use prayers composed by great men of God, because their prayers may help me, as poetry and music may, to grow in prayer. Usually, however, I find that my own words—or my own silence—say best what I need to say. As others do, I make lists of people to remind me to pray for them. The lists are certainly useful if your memory is as bad as mine is. This is not to give God reminders, but to keep my own love and care fresh and wide-ranging. In prayer we need to be stretched, but we can really pray only for those we care about sincerely. Spontaneity and freshness are vital.

I find that my prayer must always come round again to love and confidence in God, or else, even in facing and praying about the vast problems of the world, I may be disoriented by them. Disoriented men and women cannot serve their neighbors effectively and lovingly. As we long to become more truly human and so to help others to be more human, we need to reflect on the words of Isaiah—prophet and politician:

Thou dost keep in peace men of constant mind,
 in peace because they trust in thee.
Trust in the Lord for ever,
 for the Lord himself is an everlasting rock.

Intercession

Because intercession bristles with problems for many who pray, perhaps I should say a little more about praying for others.

119

Clearly, Jesus expected His followers to intercede and to persevere in interceding, yet even Jesus experienced unanswered prayer. "Simon, Simon, I have prayed that your faith may not fail." That night it failed, although later on, it is true, Peter's faith was renewed.

To begin to understand intercession we need to remind ourselves that God, who has given us freedom, often waits for our collaboration in order to achieve His purposes. For example, under normal circumstances, in healing a sick person God waits for the doctor and nurse and patient to work together with Him. If God waits for our collaboration in action, may He not wait for our collaboration in prayer? His deep purpose is to awaken and to increase our love. The healing of the paralyzed man, who was brought on a stretcher to our Lord by friends, is like a parable of intercession. While all the healing came from Jesus, humanly speaking, it looks as if the man would not have been healed unless his friends had both confidence in Christ and enough love for their friend to make the effort to bring him to the Lord.

A real question for us if we are going to intercede is: How much do we care? A story is told of Thomas Shepard, a Pilgrim Father and founder of Harvard University, who was praying for a friend apparently near death. A voice seemed to say to him, "Are you in earnest in what you ask? Would you consent to transfer to your sick friend the half of your remaining years?"

We need, therefore, to care about the people we pray about. Obviously, we cannot have affectionate feelings for all, yet Jesus says "Love your enemies and pray for your persecutors." In what sense can we love them? We can try to understand why they are what they are. We could, given the opportunity, try to help them to become truly human, the kind of men and women God wishes them to be. If we can love in that way, we can pray sincerely for them.

Perhaps intercession is one of those mysteries in life which we are wise to accept even though we may not be able to know exactly "how it works." Some very intelligent people can still say in traditional language, "We place our desires and prayers before God and, as He sees best, He sends answers to those we pray for." But there are others—many of them sincere Christians—who cannot use that kind of language. In the modern pluralistic world we have to learn to speak about many things, including the reality of intercession, in different languages, in different forms of thought. Let me try, then, to express intercession in a different idiom, not too abstrusely or clumsily, I hope.

We must face, however briefly, two basic questions: who is God? and who, or rather what, prays?

God is certainly the Lord over all, ourselves and the whole world, but He is also, as we have said repeatedly, deep within us. Therefore, when we are praying, not only are we speaking to Someone who is beyond us, but God Himself is working deep within us, changing us from inside.

What prays? Our lips pray perhaps, but not only our lips. Our minds pray also, giving meaning to our words. Our hearts pray at a deep level, because in prayer we are concerned, we care, we love. Is there a still deeper level?

When you are walking with a close friend in the country, you often have much to talk about. Sometimes you don't feel like saying much, yet, as you walk, you feel a sense of communion, deep and real. Prayer can be like that, only more so. God touches us in prayer at a far deeper level than the rather superficial self which normally shows up in the world. That is the depth, I believe, at which we can by intuition and in other ways touch one another. John Donne may have had that in mind when he wrote: "No man is an island, entire of itself; Every man is a piece of a continent, a part of the main." It is like the fact that Britain was always part of Europe, long before she entered the Common Market! The land across which primitive tribesmen once walked was swallowed up ages ago in the North Sea and deep links with Europe were, unfortunately, obliterated and forgotten.

It will help us to understand intercession, if we consider our deep human interconnectedness a little further. That wordless intuitive sensitivity which we have, or can have, with one another is probably a sign of it. I think it springs from what psychologists call our collective unconscious, "that living communion at the unconscious level which all mankind undoubtedly enjoys, even though contemporary individualistic western man has forgotten it." In my opinion, this human interrelatedness has a divine purpose as well as a natural one, for it seems to be the level at which, dynamically, God interpenetrates all.

That is my alternative language in which to talk about intercession. It is at this deep level that God sensitizes us and means his love to flow through us and permeate all humanity. It is from those depths that God means love to well up, to bring joy to our families and friends, to bring genuine caring for the underprivileged, to bring fraternity, love-in-action, among the nations. No loving less deep than that will in the end be truly effective. When we really intercede, that is what we are doing. We are opening ourselves to God and to the flow of his love. We are beginning to open ourselves to those for whom we are praying. We are touching them at a deep level. As we do that, we become authentic, we become our real selves, we become what we were made to be, human transmitters of the flow of God's love.

To use an inadequate analogy from physics, God's purpose is that his love may be like an electric current running through and warming up all humanity. Unfortunately, we all have a tendency to become self-sufficient and egotistical, like insulating blocks of mica. When we truly intercede, God is at work inside us transforming us from mica into highly conductive copper wire. We can then put no limit to how far God's energizing love may flow through us to others. "Intercession is communion with God for others."

We see again the importance of the depth of our abiding in God, our closeness to God. There are varying degrees of intimacy with God, as there are in human closeness. With the people we meet from time to time in a supermarket, we are nodding acquaintances. With others we have good relationships at work; we are closer to them. With yet others we are really close as friends, as fiancés, as partners in marriage. With God we need an ever-deepening closeness, if his love is to flow through us in prayer and in action, to our friends and to the wider world.

The New Testament uses a variety of images to convey our deepening relationship with God and with one another. We read of Christ, the Word of God, the disclosure of God, as the one who "enlightens every man," even those who are unaware of it, even, presumably, those who deny God. That cannot mean, or cannot only mean, intellectual enlightenment. It is rather God's touching and using "that living communion at the unconscious level." That is the embryonic unity of mankind, the background of confidence for all our struggles for human justice and human community.

For a deeper, a more intimate relationship with God, the New Testament uses other imagery. It speaks of Christians having the Holy Spirit dwelling in them. The Holy Spirit is, the New Testament says, ready to dwell in us. He comes in all His fullness as a result of all that Jesus did in His life of service and love, in His facing death, in His rising again to pour new energies of love into His followers. We have now only to open our hearts by faith, by confidence in Him. These energies are the power of the Holy Spirit. It is the Holy Spirit who desires to unite Christians to one another as the Body of Christ and the Bride of Christ. So we come to Paul's profound prayer in his letter to the Ephesians: "May God grant you strength and power through his Spirit in your inner being, that through faith Christ may dwell in your hearts in love." That helps us to understand a little clearer what intercession means. Through the Holy Spirit, the Risen Christ dwells in our hearts. He is now—to use another New Testament image—the Christ "who ever lives to make intercession." We must not take that image, or any other image, naively, as literal description. Clearly, we must not think that intercession is just "one of the things" that the Risen Christ does in heaven. His intercession is the continuing resultant of all He has done for us in His loving us, even when uncompromising love meant that He had to face death, and in His passing through death to the eternal glory of heaven as the victory of love. In a very real sense, it is not so much that Christ intercedes but that His presence in the glory of heaven *is* His intercession. As it says in the letter to the Hebrews, "He appears now before God on our behalf." Because this is so, we too, who are members of the body of the interceding Christ, are to "appear before God in union with Christ on behalf of our fellow men and women." "To intercede is," as Archbishop Michael Ramsey has said, "to be in Jesus, to be with God with those whom we love in our heart."

Intercession is, however, not only the desires of hearts and the words of prayer. Intercession means for us, as it meant for Christ the great intercessor, ourselves, given to God to be channels of His love to the world. We are called to be not merely intercessors, but "living intercessions." Oliver C. Quick, a most perceptive theologian, has put it this way:

> True intercession must spring from a love and a desire to help the person for whom we pray. Thus intercession is *a representative dedication* to God of the total help which we give or desire to give, constantly and in varying forms, to the person for whom we intercede. . . . Our understanding leads us up to wider interpretations of the nature of prayer whereby religious thinkers ancient and modern have extended its range far beyond those times in which we consciously set ourselves to pray. It will follow that the secular activities of our life will constitute the very substance and matter of what we offer in prayer.

Intercession and life are to become one.

Learning by doing

Prayer, I hope you see, is so wide and profound an activity that we shall never cease to explore and to learn.

The only way to learn to swim is by swimming, the only way to learn to love is by loving, the only way to learn to pray is by praying. Books on prayer, conferences on prayer, advice on prayer, may well be useful, but they cannot take the place of praying and going on and on with praying.

One of the greatest helps with praying is to make a retreat. I suggest that a retreat each year is the fourth essential for the average man and woman who wishes to pray seriously, in addition to the quiet time of openness to God in the mornings, the turning to God in the evenings, and the weekly worship, if possible, at the Eucharist.

Of course, a retreat is not possible for everyone—young couples with families, for example. They might receive some help in the life of prayer from visits *en famille* to religious community centers.

It was my first retreat in silence, as I said at the beginning of this book, which was a great turning point in my own life. Since then, I have each year been able to make my own retreat, many of which have been milestones in my journey. In my vocation I am asked to conduct retreats in different countries for varied kinds of people. Whenever I lead a retreat, I try to participate in it, and many have been times of insight and strengthening for me. In retreat we find quietness, leisure, and openness to God and to love. We are not so much instructed as encouraged to pray, to explore for ourselves what prayer is.

Through all seasons

Friends, lovers, partners in marriage, know they have to go through all sorts of seasons together. It is that which deepens and strengthens their friendship and love. It is the same with prayer, with the prayer that makes us more richly human. While I have found that there are more fresh spring days in the life of prayer than I expected, we have to make up our minds that we are going on, hail, rain, or snow.

We are in good company.

Thomas More was a man of prayer but no recluse, wealthy, twice-married, warm, urbane, scholar among scholars, Lord Chancellor, first statesman in the realm of Henry VIII. Some distance from his house by the Thames at Chelsea, he built the "New Building," and there, early—morning by morning, "he occupied himself with prayer and study." That was the hidden spring of his charm, of his love, and of his steel-like strength. No one could shift him on a point of conscience. Although he was sent to the Tower, he maintained his discipline of prayer, and never lost his warmth. He sent a last note to his dearest daughter after their final parting, "I never liked your manner towards me better than when you kissed me last. Farewell, my dear child, and pray for me, as I will for you and all your friends." He went resolutely to the scaffold, claiming to be to the end "the King's good servant, but God's servant first."

Dietrich Bonhoeffer, son of the finest liberal Protestant culture in Berlin, saw more quickly than others the evil of Nazism. On this issue, he parted from the majority of his fellow German Protestants. He took the lead in the Confessing Church and trained future ministers in a clandestine seminary on the Baltic coast. His book, *Life Together*, is his legacy, how he rooted these heroic men in authentic disciplined prayer. He did not shrink from plotting the assassination of Hitler. The life of prayer that gave him that toughness, he continued in his prison cell. "When I wake up about 6 a.m. I like to read a few psalms and hymns, think about you all and remember that you are thinking about me," he wrote to his aged parents and his fiancée. Just before his execution a fellow prisoner, an agnostic English officer, wrote, "Bonhoeffer always seemed to me to diffuse an atmosphere of happiness, of joy in every smallest event of life and of deep gratitude for the mere fact that he was alive. He was one of the very few men that I have ever met to whom his God was real and close to him."

Edward Wilson, doctor and ornithologist, went with Scott to the South Pole. During the voyage, on a ship crowded with men and equipment, he used to climb early each morning to the lookout place on the mast. He wrote to his wife at home, "I simply love the crow's nest. It is not very warm in a bitter wind, but as private as can be and therefore a very easy place to find you and I just love it for my daily prayers and reading with you." He was the life of the party on board ship. Later on, as they were dying together in a lonely tent on the Great Ice Barrier, Scott wrote to Wilson's wife, "He is everlastingly cheerful, ready to sacrifice himself for others and never a word of blame for me for leading him into this mess."

We share life in mind and heart with those men of prayer. We face the world of our own day with its potentialities and all its crying needs. Our paths will not be the same, but together we want to discover for others and for ourselves—and it is more than the task of a lifetime—how to become fully human. We are mere apprentices in love.

FOR FURTHER READING

Abishiktananda, *Prayer.* Philadelphia, Pa.: Westminster Press, 1973.

Bloom, Anthony, *God and Man.* Paramus, N.J.: Paulist/ Newman Press, 1973.

Teilhard de Chardin, Pierre, *Divine Milieu.* New York: Harper & Row, Publishers, 1960.

Dalrymple, John, *The Christian Affirmation.* London: Darton, Longman & Todd, 1971.

Dodd, C. H., *Founder of Christianity.* New York: Macmillan Company, 1970.

Drury, John, *Angels and Dirt.* London: Darton, Longman & Todd, 1972.

Farrer, Austin M., *Love Almighty and Ills Unlimited.* London: William Collins Sons & Co., Ltd., 1966 (A Fontana book).

Gibbard, Mark, *Why Pray?* Valley Forge, Pa.: Judson Press, 1971.

Macquarrie, John, *God and Secularity.* London: Lutterworth Press, 1968.

Shaw, D. W. D., *Who Is God?* London: SCM Press, 1968.

Ward, J. N., *The Use of Praying.* London: Epworth Press, 1967.